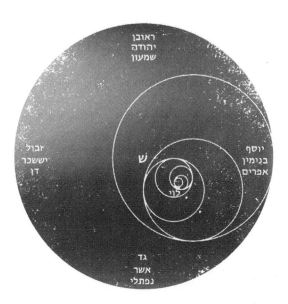

HASHAMAYIM 1A
Adonijah O. Ogbonnaya, PhD
Copyright © 2015 Adonijah O. Ogbonnaya, PhD

Front Cover Illustration by Taylor Remington

Published by Seraph Creative in 2015
United States / United Kingdom / South Africa / Australia
www.seraphcreative.org

Typesetting, Illustration & Layout by Feline
www.felinegraphics.com

Aactev8
1020 Victoria Ave, Venice, California
www.aactev8.com

First printed in the United States of America

ISBN: 978-0-9944335-0-3

HASHAMAYIM 1A

ANGELS, HEAVENLY STRUCTURES & THE SONS OF GOD

By

ADONIJAH O. OGBONNAYA, PHD

Published by Seraph Creative

CONTENTS

FOREWORD

Adonijah is one of the best theological, mystical teachers that, in my opinion, is on the face of the earth. His work carries with it an authority and grace drawn not from the knowledge of men through study but from a very poignant relationship with YHVH, carrying the full authentic background of the Messianic Hebrew culture.

His depth of understanding of Scripture is profound and is authenticated by his encounters in the realms of the Father. Anyone engaging in his materials will have their mind bent to the breaking point until surrendering to the unfathomable depth of the love of YHSVH.

I would recommend them to anyone willing to learn about who the Sons of God really are.

In His service,

Ian Clayton

Son Of Thunder

PUBLISHER'S NOTE

I do not know the costs of being a forerunner personally but I have met many men and women who have walked in realities of Christ decades before the church was ready to embrace them. There is certainly a great cost personally, relationally, professionally and even financially paid by such trail blazers, who have laid down everything for the revelation of Christ and His Kingdom. Adonijah Ogbonnaya, affectionately known as Dr O, is one of these people.

It is a great honor to be trusted with such material by Dr O and the Father. HaShamayim truly reveals Heaven's heart for Earth. In reading this book I trust you will be as changed in your understanding of the greatness of God, and the access he has granted the born again believer, as we were in the process of publishing.

So, firstly, thank-you to Dr O and the Aactev8 team who worked so closely on the making of the HaShamayim series and trusted us with the fruit of your intimacy with the Creator.

Secondly, to you the reader, congratulations on picking up this book. No one comes to the Son unless the Father draws them. May you discover and become who you already are - a Son of God.

HOW TO USE THIS BOOK

In your hands you are holding a man's life. The HaShamayim series is the result of decades of intimacy and pursuit of a man for his Creator.

From years spent with God and the scriptures Dr O has accessed dimensions of the heavenly realms through, the work of Christ. With great clarity and vulnerability Dr O has opened his understanding for the hungry. Accordingly, may what cost him 30 years take you 3, as God opens your heart to the great things he has prepared for you.

This is not a book to be intellectually understood and categorized. It is a doorway to experiencing the person God, and thus yourself, in greater and greater truth. Please take your time in marinating and meditating on the scriptures and revelation contained in this book. Ask Holy Spirit to reveal to you the deep realities behind the printed words. He surely will.

Also, we have worked hard to produce illustrations to help the reader gain an accurate grid for what is being presented - but even the best diagram will not come close to conveying the wonder of encountering the multi-faceted wisdom of God and His created dimensions for yourself. All glory to Him!

Go higher. Go deeper. Enjoy. It is the Father's delight to give you the Kingdom - so let us go boldly through the New and Living Way.

Great Peace,

The Seraph Creative Team

ACKNOWLEDGEMENTS

I asked God for the words to share the vision I have when I look at you :

"You hold within your frame a divine purpose. When I interact with you, I am shown a marvelous mystery. I am graced with a glimpse of revelation.

You are the form of mystery. You are the reason for revelation. You are the wonder of worlds. You are the image of the Creator - a visible image of the unseen."

I especially want to thank my wife Benedicta Ogbonnaya, who has walked this path with me for 36 years. Her patience, love, strength and wisdom have touched the lives of many and she has most profoundly blessed my life.

I want to thank all of my students worldwide for your support over the years.

Taylor and Megan Remington, you are more than just my students. I am honored to call you my friends and co-laborers.

Thank you to Helen Staley who transcribed the lectures and made this book possible.

Thank you Zachary Wernli for your continued enthusiastic input on the production of this series.

Thank you Seraph Creative for catching our heart, carrying our message and working with excellence.

May God richly bless you all.

Dr O

PREFACE

The mystery of the Christian faith is encapsulated in the firm belief that God became human in Christ without diminishing God's divinity nor dissolving humanity. Now, in one man we find the complete presence of God and humanity. Jesus tells us over and over again that he came down from heaven and speaks of heaven more than he speaks of many of the ideas with which we are so easily occupied. Jesus says to us that He is the one who "descended from heaven, even the Son of Man" (John 3:13 NAS).

Furthermore, He says, "I have come down from heaven" (John 6:38 NAS). By his discourse on heaven he is pointing us to look into the heavens or at least to find out what it looks like. He does not stop there. Jesus tells us that we who belong to him are born from heaven. This in itself is an invitation to enter the mysteries of heaven. I believe we live in an age where this hunger for entering into the heavens and seeing the marvels of those realms will increase. To me, the primary purpose of the coming of Jesus into the world is to open the gates and the door to the heavenly dimension, for me and for all of humanity. The true message of Christianity then is that the door to the heavens has opened to all who, by their freewill, choose to believe the Messiah whom God has sent in the Person of Yeshua (Jesus) HaMashiach (The Christ). The acceptance or being in Him is an activation of dynamic relationship of the universe within the human person and the larger universe of God - who is the all encompassing reality. His coming means that we are no longer cut off from God and that the microcosm is no longer separated from the macrocosm.

Heaven has become a great interest to those of us who have been born from above and are reaching for intimacy with God through Jesus Christ. This interest has become more pronounced not just by the many 'born again' but also by many in the world. This interest is spurring a new kind of "ascension mystical theology". Something that may be called by some scholars "apocalyptic mysticism". Whatever the name, this renewed interest in understanding - or least having a glimpse to what heaven looks like - is more likely to keep increasing than to wane.

In my journey towards understanding who I am in the Father through the Son, Jesus Christ, I have had many experiences whose examination and analysis, instead of proffering final solutions to intractable spiritual questions, has rather fuelled more burning questions. So rather than offer you a final answer to your questions about the heavens, I hope this book spurs you to ask more questions and to press into the heavens and to search the Scriptures to find more of what the Father has for us as God's Children.

If a believer is born from above (heaven, John 3:16), is it not logical then that the believer should return there as often as he or she desires or is able? If the believer, the one who is born from above, is seated in the heavenlies, as Paul so succinctly put in Ephesians, does it not call forth a need to understand what the heavens looks like? I began very early in my journey to ask for understanding of how heaven is structured and also to seek for a language on how to narrate my experiences. These experiences are the results of my travel to the heavens through the technology of the person of Jesus who is the way and door to enter those realms of heaven.

My approach to the heavens in this book is simple: to look at the organization and the structure of the children of Israel around the house of God in the wilderness as a microcosmic manifestation of the macrocosmic. It is a picture, if you may, of aspects of the heavens. Though I have had visions and have been carried in the spirit into what I consider to be the heavens, I could not just accept my flight of vision or imagination as proof of its reality. I had to search the Scriptures. I also looked at what the Apostle John narrated within his Apocalypse/Revelation and other hints within the text of Scripture to form at least a reasonable base for my description of the structures of heaven. I therefore searched the Scriptures and found that it has painted for us in many places what the heavens look like. This is just my simple offering to members of the Body of Christ based on the interpretation of my experience as I see it through Scripture.

> **"** Though I have had visions and have being carried in the spirit into what I consider to be the heavens, I could not just accept my flight of vision or imagination as proof of its reality. **"**

This is the first of what will be a three-part set on the heavens. May the Lord use it to bless you.

Shalom
Adonijah O. Ogbonnaya
Venice CA
2015

INTRODUCTION

This book is the study of the twelve lower structures of the twelve houses of the City of God, revealed to John in the Apocalypse (Revelation 21). The study of the twelve houses of Israel will affect how you see, grasp, and understand the structures of Heaven, or what has been called by the Apostle John, the City of God. This substance of the spiritual world is meant to transform our life here on earth and radically transform the way we see God, the world, ourselves, matter, reality and the way we operate in our day-to-day lives.

An understanding of the structures of Heaven is meant to turn right-side up how we interact with and view the world. Moreover, its ongoing transformation is constantly happening before our eyes. An understanding of the heavenly structures and the processes found there can also help you to begin to grasp your body, your soul, and your spirit, and give you a glimpse of the inter-relationship of everything.

Getting to know the structures and dimensions of heaven ties many of the things spoken of in Scripture together. Everything spoken of in Scripture - cherubim, seraphim, angels, heaven and hell, soul, spirit and even demons - are connected in a very special way. If we pay attention, we will notice that these are not anomalies but the very basic fabric of Christian spirituality.

To begin to enter these dimensions we must overcome the disease of restlessness and sit still and know - both from the text and from the inner experience of the Spirit and even early Christian tradition - and practice engaging the presence. It is the practice of the presence and inward looking, informed by the revelation of the Word, which will allow you to enter into certain places and gates depicted by the book of Revelation.

To move in these dimensions as believers, we must be still and "know that I am God" (Psa 46:10). This knowing that "I am God" is a two way street for the believer. Firstly, it entails God looking inside where Christ dwells in the heart. Secondly, we are looking at God to see who we are in God through the prism of Christ who sits in the inner chambers of our heart. We also need to know what God has communicated about Himself and how to key into it. 'Knowledge' and 'being' are connected in true intimacy with God.

Introduction

SECTION 1:

ANGELS AND HEAVENLY STRUCTURES

For most Christians 'heaven' is an abstract concept - the place you go when you die. It houses the Trinity, a huge throne, some angels and maybe your dead aunty.

Heaven is actually a series of interconnected dimensions - more accurately describes as 'the heavens' - that God wants you to discover right now. God created the heavens for the very reason that you could experience Him, know Him and become like Him. The heavens were made for you.

These heavenly dimensions are your home, the place you were born. Understanding the nature of these heavens and how they relate to each other, and to yourself, is key to starting your journey of discovering all God has for you - and revealing who you truly are.

THE NEW JERUSALEM

Here is our key text. Please take your time to read, imagine and meditate on it. We will refer back to this text all through the book.

₁ The first heaven and the first earth passed away, and there is no longer *any* sea.

² And I saw the holy city, New Jerusalem, coming down out of heaven from God, made ready as a bride adorned for her husband.

₃ And I heard a loud voice from the throne, saying, "Behold, the tabernacle of God is among men, and He shall dwell among them, and they shall be His people, and God Himself shall be among them,

₄ and He shall wipe away every tear from their eyes; and there shall no longer be *any* death; there shall no longer be *any* mourning, or crying, or pain; the first things have passed away.

₅ And He who sits on the throne said, "Behold, I am making all things new." And He said, "Write, for these words are faithful and true."

₆ And He said to me, "It is done. I am the Alpha and the Omega, the beginning and the end. I will give to the one who thirsts from the spring of the water of life without cost.

₇ "He who overcomes shall inherit these things, and I will be his God and he will be My son.

₈ "But for the cowardly and unbelieving and abominable and murderers and immoral persons and sorcerers and idolaters and all liars, their part *will be* in the lake that burns with fire and brimstone, which is the second death.

₉ And one of the seven angels who had the seven bowls full of the seven last plagues, came and spoke with me, saying, "Come here, I shall show you the bride, the wife of the Lamb."

₁₀ And he carried me away in the Spirit to a great and high mountain, and showed me the holy city, Jerusalem, coming down out of heaven from God,

₁₁ having the glory of God. Her brilliance was like a very costly stone, as a stone of crystal-clear jasper.

₁₂ It had a great and high wall, with twelve gates, and at the gates twelve angels; and names were written on them, which are *those* of the twelve tribes of the sons of Israel.

₁₃ *There were* three gates on the east and three gates on the north and three gates on the south and three gates on the west.

₁₄ And the wall of the city had twelve foundation

stones, and on them *were* the twelve names of the twelve apostles of the Lamb.

15 And the one who spoke with me had a gold measuring rod to measure the city, and its gates and its wall.

16 And the city is laid out as a square, and its length is as great as the width; and he measured the city with the rod, fifteen hundred miles; its length and width and height are equal.

17 And he measured its wall, seventy-two yards, *according* to human measurements, which are *also* angelic *measurements.*

18 And the material of the wall was jasper; and the city was pure gold, like clear glass.

19 The foundation stones of the city wall were adorned with every kind of precious stone. The first foundation stone was jasper; the second, sapphire; the third, chalcedony; the fourth, emerald;

20 the fifth, sardonyx; the sixth, sardius; the seventh, chrysolite; the eighth, beryl; the ninth, topaz; the tenth, chrysoprase; the eleventh, jacinth; the twelfth, amethyst.

21 And the twelve gates were twelve pearls; each one of the gates was a single pearl. And the street of the city was pure gold, like transparent glass.

22 And I saw no temple in it, for the Lord God, the Almighty, and the Lamb, are its temple.

$_{23}$ And the city has no need of the sun or of the moon to shine upon it, for the glory of God has illumined it, and its lamp is the Lamb.

$_{24}$ And the nations shall walk by its light, and the kings of the earth shall bring their glory into it.

$_{25}$ And in the daytime (for there shall be no night there) its gates shall never be closed;

$_{26}$ and they shall bring the glory and the honor of the nations into it;

$_{27}$ and nothing unclean and no one who practices abomination and lying, shall ever come into it, but only those whose names are written in the Lamb's book of life. (Rev 21:1-27 NAS)

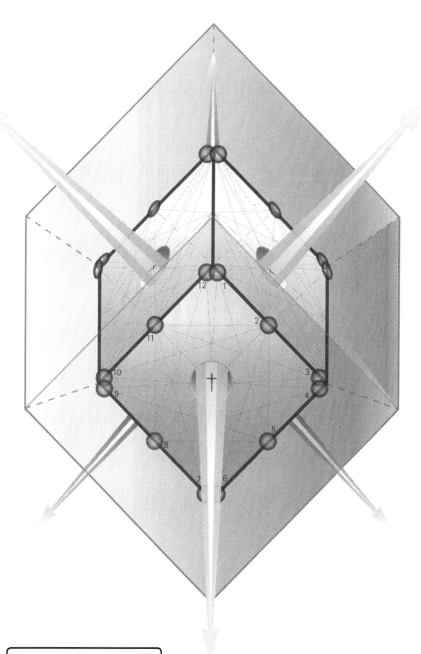

THE NEW JERUSALEM

DISCOVERING THE MYSTICAL

When we receive a gift or favor we accept along with it the responsibility to guard it. Before we can properly teach and disseminate what we have received, we need to delve deeply into it and make sure that it has marinated in our thoughts. It is never advisable to begin teaching people about anything we have not first grasped for ourselves. We need to be clear about what part of the topic we have grasped and what still eludes us. How much do we grasp of its depths? What is our limitation as far as the subject matter is concerned?

> **"** It is imperative that we pay close attention to the little details of the spiritual experiences that we have along the way in this journey of life - especially our life in Christ - for in them we find God's call bidding us towards a closer relationship with Him. **"**

Before writing this book about the structures of Heaven, I had to come to terms with the fact that no matter how much vision and insight one has into the things of the spirit, "we know in part and prophesy in part" (1 Cor 13:9). Because I am keenly aware of this, I really had to delve deeply into the subject and work on some things that required me to pay attention to my own limitations and inner struggles.

It is imperative that we pay close attention to the little details of the spiritual experiences that we have along the way in this journey of life - especially our life in Christ - for in them we find God's call bidding us towards a closer relationship with Him.

The experiences of those who call themselves by the name of Christ must be examined in order to determine if they correlate with the revelation that the LORD has given in the various images, structures and processes used in Scripture. These structures and processes communicate spiritual knowledge to God's people, in all the covenants He has made, for the benefit of all those who will seek His face.

I focused my attention on how God structured His interaction with the people of Israel, knowing that this relationship serves as an interpretive archetype for making sense of the secret things of God on Earth. For years I had paid attention to my own inner experiences, visions, and dreams. I sought the Lord for an understanding of that which the church, for some reason, has either forgotten to tell me or neglected to tell me.

The more I have paid attention to the way God interacts with me and how it fits with the Scriptures, the more I have come to the conclusion that the Scriptures are no mere letter to be preached. Rather, they carry within them God-codes for understanding and grasping the structures of His divine interaction with humanity along with the methods and means for experiencing the heavens. Yes, even the whole universe.

The more attention I paid to the Word of God as that which encapsulates divine mysteries, the more I found them to be escalators for "going up and down" between heaven and earth and "in and out" of the dimensions of the heavenlies. I concluded that we who seek God could not afford to ignore the spiritual mysteries represented in the Word of God. We could no longer ignore the symbols and codes in Scriptures, which speak sometimes in veiled terms regarding the Kingdom of God and the Kingdom of heaven.

What was going on in my life for years was different from what I had been told in church and what I had been taught during my ten years of theological education. How do I explain that as a young business apprentice in Jos, Nigeria, at the end of that fasting and prayer for many days, I felt myself being lifted up from the ground? Yes, "levitation."

With my focus centered on Jesus Christ, I had spoken in tongues for several hours. I was above the ground about three feet. There was no fear while this was happening. It was a gentle lifting up, not a violent wind. This experience lasted about five minutes.

I know that this was not demonic. One cannot spend hours calling on the LORD and upon Jesus Christ the Son and then be answered by a demon. For it is written, "Call unto me and I will answer thee" (Jer 33:3). Notice it is "I" the LORD, not another. If I call on the LORD Jesus Christ and a demon answers, then for some reason, the demon has become the fulfiller of the promise of God. God forbid! If we call on the LORD, He will answer us. That is the guarantee we have from the LORD.

I also know it was not a dream. As gently as I was lifted up, I was calmly put back on the ground where I was seated. Only then did a strange sense of awe grasp me. I did not tell this experience to anyone for fear of being condemned.

The second experience occurred while I was a doctoral student at Claremont School of Theology. After hours of studying I went home from the library to rest. As was my custom I decided to pray before going to bed. I sat down to meditate and, as soon as I began speaking and singing in tongues, I felt a shift in the room.

I did not give full attention to what seemed to me at that moment to have been wind from an open window. I chose to open my eyes while I kept my whole focus still upon the image of Christ on the throne before my mind's eye. I noticed that I was once again lifted up from the ground. However, this time I saw as though a window had opened, allowing me to view my Father's house - seeing what was going on there as if I was actually there myself.

> " I saw that its spiritual heritage had been stolen, perverted by the so-called occult and new age. I felt this need to release the people of Christ to experience and interact with the spiritual dimensions, which Christians so often open in their worship, yet they seldom activate its power for personal and communal transformation. "

From my Father's house I was carried to various cities and nations where I stood and preached to crowds of men and women and saw great transformation in their lives. I had conversations back and forth about the need to restore the mystical to the body of Christ. I saw that its spiritual heritage had been stolen, perverted by the so-called occult and new age. I felt this need to release the people of Christ to experience and interact with the spiritual dimensions, which Christians so often open in their worship, yet they seldom activate its power for personal and communal transformation.

I was then led to a throne room resembling that described by John in the book of Revelation where I heard many strange things regarding the Word of God and heralds of what will come. I was given the understanding that, as Christians begin to experience the heavens much more, a great divide will occur in every major denomination - theologically and experientially.

This divide will occur between those who begin to experience the inner mysteries of God that lead to radical transformation of both self and society and those who refuse the mysteries and insist upon adhering to their perceived sacrosanct physical structures and denominational boundaries.

When I came to myself I was at least two feet off the ground. Again, I was let down gently. Now understand my focus had been the Word of God, the person of Jesus Christ and the precious Holy Spirit, which proceeds from the Father and the Son.

JESUS IS THE LIVING DOOR

How do we get into the heavenly realms and move through the dimensions? Nothing I say in this book is intended to make anyone think that by their own power or their own righteousness they can go into the heavens. Entering heaven is a gift given freely through grace by God the Father through the Son Jesus Christ. The Lord Jesus said of Himself, "I am the way, the truth and the life. No one comes to the Father except through Me." (Jn 14:6)

> "Entering heaven is a gift given freely through grace by God the Father through the Son Jesus Christ. The Lord Jesus said of Himself, "I am the way, the truth and the life. No one comes to the Father except through Me." (Jn 14:6)"

He made it clear that He came down from the heavens while discussing with His brethren the issue of the bread of life. "For I have come down from heaven, not to do My own will, but the will of Him who sent Me. (Jn 6:38 NKJ) In another passage He stated clearly,

₇ Then Jesus said to them again, "Most assuredly, I say to you, I am the door of the sheep. ₈ "All who *ever* came before Me are thieves and robbers, but the sheep did not hear them. ₉ "I am the door. If anyone enters by Me, he will be saved, and will go in and out and find pasture. ₁₀ "The thief does not come except to steal, and to kill, and to destroy. I have come that they may have life, and that they may have *it* more abundantly. ₁₁ "I am the good shepherd. The good shepherd gives His life for the sheep. (Jn 10:7 - 11 NKJ).

That the Lord Jesus is the door means that entrance into heaven is only granted through Him. Christ came to grant man the opportunity to enter, or rather re-enter, into paradise and therefore have access into the heavens again. The key to this lies in the atoning sacrifice which He freely made with His own life.

If you are reading this book I assume that you have passed this place and are fully planted into the life of the Lord Jesus. If not, you may want to make that choice now. Without Him, you may be trafficking in the demonic inadvertently. For any of us to have access to and to navigate within the heavenly realm, engaging it for the transformation of our life in creation, we must first know Jesus Christ as the way, the truth and the life. We must be certain within our heart that we have been crucified with Christ (Rom. 6:6). We must hold firmly the testimony of the shed blood of Jesus Christ. It is only by the shedding of the blood of the Son of God that we have salvation.

₁₉ Since therefore, brethren, we have confidence to enter the holy place by the blood of Jesus, for He has given us. ₂₀ a new and living way which He inaugurated

for us through the veil, that is, His flesh [21] and since *we have* a great priest over the House of God, [22] let us draw near with a sincere heart in full assurance of faith, having our hearts sprinkled *clean* from an

> **"** On our part, we must come with a heart full of assurance of faith. Our hearts must be sprinkled by the blood, resulting in the removal of an evil conscience. Our bodies must be washed with pure water (the Word of God). **"**

evil conscience and our bodies washed with pure water. (Heb 10:19-22 NAS)

According to the above passage, we can only enter the heavens and especially the place where the throne of the LORD dwells by "a new and living way" and not by the old and dead way of the flesh. Three things define this new and living way. Only through these three can one enter the heavens, for they open the gate of the heavenlies to the believer: 1) the blood of Jesus Christ; 2) the veil of His flesh; 3) His priesthood.

On our part, we must come with a heart full of assurance of faith. Our hearts must be sprinkled by the blood, resulting in the removal of an evil conscience. Our bodies must be washed with pure water (the Word of God).

ACCESS BY THE BLOOD

You are seated in the heavenlies with Christ. The Scriptures state the Father "hath raised *us* up together, and made *us* sit together in heavenly *places* in Christ Jesus" (Eph 2:6). The purpose of this raising into the heavenlies is that the principalities and powers that are in the heavenlies, who have occupied the places rightly belonging to man created in the image and likeness of God, might learn wisdom because of our fall.

"To the intent that now unto the principalities and powers in heavenly *places* might be known by the church the manifold wisdom of God," (Eph. 3:10).

> **"** We are not talking here of the natural man trying to reach heaven by his pitiful power or through the crafting of his fallen will. **"**

This has always been "the eternal purpose which He (God) purposed in Christ Jesus our Lord" (Eph 3:11) - that we should have access to the heavenlies and operate from that vantage point as we implement the purpose of God upon the earth and, if you may, upon all created realms. This "boldness" to access the heavens with confidence only comes from the faith of Him (Jesus Christ) "in whom we have boldness and access with confidence by the faith of Him" (Eph 3:10-12).

We are not talking here of the natural man trying to reach heaven by his pitiful power or through the crafting of his fallen will. Rather, we are speaking of that:

20 Which He wrought in Christ, when God raised Him from the dead, and set *Him* at God's own right hand in the heavenly *places*, (heavens) 21 Far above all principality, and power, and might, and dominion, and every name that is named, not only in this world, but also in that which is to come: 22 And hath put all *things* under His feet, and gave Him *to be* the head over all *things* to the church 23 Which is His body, the fullness of Him that filleth all in all. (Eph 1:20-23)

Those who have known Jesus Christ and been filled with the Holy Spirit are partakers of the calling of the heavens. That is, all things celestial resound with their new name. The way to understand this partaking in the voice of the heavenlies is to consider two things:

1. The apostleship of Jesus Christ - an apostle is one who is sent to trail blaze and to open the closed paths.

2. His high priestly office - a priest is one who mediates between dimensions to allow flows of treasures and exchanges between them.

In Israel, the High Priest who walked in the ordinances of God was the only one who entered the Holy of Holies. He was able to navigate the reality of the heavenlies, represented by the shadow of things outside of the heavenly Holy of Holies. This stepping into the heavenlies was accomplished by the temporary satisfaction offered by the blood of animals.

When Jesus entered into the heavenlies by His blood, He opened the realities of the heavenlies for those who participate by faith in the applied blood that was shed. Therefore, it is written:

"Wherefore, holy brethren, partakers of the heavenly calling, consider the Apostle and High Priest of our profession, Christ Jesus" (Heb 3:1).

I even want to venture to state that those who walk in the heavenlies are:

1) Those who have been enlightened by the Holy Spirit

2) Those who have tasted the heavenly gift by entering into the heavens and been shown the mysteries of that realm

3) They are those who are partakers of the Holy Spirit and the four rivers of Eden having made their habitation in them (as the Lord said, "out of their belly flow rivers of living waters")

4) They are those who have tasted the good Word of God

5) They have also tasted the power of the world to come. These believers are they whose backsliding is irreversible.

> ₄For *it is* impossible for those who were once enlightened, and have tasted of the heavenly gift, and were made partakers of the Holy Ghost, ₅And have tasted the good word of God, and the powers of the world to come, If they shall fall away, to renew them again unto repentance; seeing they crucify to themselves the Son of God afresh, and put him to an open shame. (Heb 6:4-6)

ACCESSING BY THE NAME OF GOD

We are now going to deal with a powerful key for activating certain heavens and certain dimensions of heaven within the divine. One of the things the Bible is very clear about is the letters of God's name: Yod י, Heh ה. Vav ו Heh ה. These letters are a key to unlocking that dimension when God is moving in a certain heaven.

Psalm 148:1 "Praise ye the Lord! Praise ye the Lord from the heavens" Remember, the Lord is always this four-letter word. It is "Yod-Heh-Vav-Heh". The reason the capitals 'L-O-R-D' are used in some translations of the Bible is to represent the four-letter name of God, YHVH. Therefore, the L-O-R-D represents the Yod-Heh-Vav-Heh. "Praise ye the LORD! Praise ye the LORD from the heavens."

HEH	VAV	HEH	YOD

The name of God in Hebrew, read right to left.

Now I want to make something clear before we move ahead. LORD is written twice in the Psalm 148 passage. That is four plus four, equaling 8. This is the music key - the octave. Yod-Heh-Vav-Heh, Yod-Heh-Vav-Heh. It is the octave, completing the circle of the sound.

You cannot access these heavens without sound. Sound is more than spoken words, it can also be sound vibrations. The reason God gave man a voice is because it is by voice that you access the various heavens. It's by voice and sound. It says, "Praise Him in the

❚❚ We are now going to deal with a powerful key for activating certain heavens and certain dimensions of heaven within the divine. One of the things the Bible is very clear about is the letters of God's name: Yod ', Heh ה. Vav Heh. These letters are a key to unlocking that dimension when God is moving in a certain heaven. **❚❚**

heights!" It's not talking about physical mountains here.

"Praise Him, all His angels. Praise Him, all His hosts!" Can you see the repetition? "Praise ye Him, sun, and moon; Praise Him, all ye stars." Every dimension has its own sun, its own moon and its own stars. "Praise Him, you heaven of the heavens, and you waters that be above the heavens."

Here is something else that is in every heaven - a sea. The Sea of Glass is just one sea. Most of the time a heaven is mentioned, there is a sea or a river mentioned. There's a reason for that. In many places, there is also proximity of wilderness.

There is a simple pattern shown in the movement of the children of Israel. You cross the water to get into the wilderness. Then you cross the wilderness and cross another body of water in order to get into the Promised Land. It is the same structure. That is how the Egyptians themselves even looked at their kingdom. Their kingdom was based around the Nile; there are two rivers coming together.

There are waters above. "Praise him, you highest heavens and you waters above the skies. Let them praise the name of the Lord. For He commanded and they were created. He had established them forever and ever. He has made a decree which shall not pass." (Psa 148:4-5)

THE MYSTERIES OF GOD IN SCRIPTURE

Every teaching of biblical mysteries must focus on Scripture and must look at it as more than words and external facts. Everything God reveals in Scripture to Israel - the seasons, the holidays, the garments, the movements, the structures, the tribal interactions and all the sacrifices - can be looked at in terms of literal activities. However, doing only that will blind the reader to the mysteries of God, the universe, heaven, angels, and all of the spiritual possibilities they are meant to reveal.

In our day, the need to focus on Scripture and gaze intently into it until it manifests its mysteries in our life is vital. Throughout the history of humanity there have been men and women who have looked beyond the material and beyond the letter of Scripture. From that spiritual groundedness in Scripture they have been transported into another world while still in this physical dimension. Even today there are men and women who move between dimensions, who travel, look into the structures of heaven, and go to different places. (If you want greater background on what I am teaching you can go to www.aactev8.com)

Mysteries are not for babies. "As newborn babes, desire the sincere milk of the word, that ye may grow thereby" (1 Peter 2:2) and learn the fundamentals of the faith. However, for some, it is time to come up higher and go deeper into the mysteries of the person of the Lord and of the Word.

This book is for people who actually want to experience and know things that are not ordinary. It is for people who want more than a Sunday religious experience - people who desire more of God, more of the Spirit, more of the revelation of the mysteries of Jesus Christ. Now let me be clear; you do not have to believe anything I am teaching here to be saved. You only need Jesus Christ as your LORD.

There are no specially kept secrets being hidden from anyone that cannot be searched out and found. However, there are mysteries. If anyone tells you that he has a secret to teach you that is not based on the Word of God, be careful. That said, however, there are mysteries in Scripture. To deny this truth is to rob ourselves of the fuller understanding of God's gift to us and what is available to us.

The denial of Christian mysteries and the continual denial of the supernatural are what have given the occult inroads into our children and into people who have had experiences that are uncommon in our rationalistic world. There clearly are mysteries. The Apostle Paul says, "We speak mysteries among the mature." (I Cor 2:6-7) We do not speak mysteries to children.

The sickness of so much of the current church is that it has developed a dangerous aversion to mysteries. It ignores what needs to be said and goes about saying nonsense in order to avoid having to answer difficult questions about the spiritual world. Jesus tells us that one of the birthrights of the children of the Kingdom of God is to know the mysteries of the Kingdom of heaven. Matthew mentions the Kingdom of heaven, while Luke mentions the Kingdom of God. Both convey the same idea - that there are mysteries. The details of these mysteries and their explanations belong to the children of God. In spite of the previous statement it should be kept in mind that the Kingdom of God and the Kingdom of heaven are not always used in scripture with the same meaning. There is a common element which is the idea that both the Kingdom of God and Kingdom of heaven reveal

> **"** The sickness of so much of the current church is that it has developed a dangerous aversion to mysteries. It ignores what needs to be said and goes about saying nonsense in order to avoid having to answer difficult questions about the spiritual world. **"**

God as the sole and absolute sovereign and that his kingdom is the expression in creation of the reign of God - which then includes all who rule under the authority of God.

> [11] He answered and said unto them, "Because it is given unto you to know the mysteries of the Kingdom of heaven, but to them it is not given." (Matt 13:11)

> [10] And he said, "Unto you it is given to know the mysteries of the Kingdom of God, but to others in parables; that seeing they might not see, and hearing they might not understand." (Luke 8:10)

It is good to note that while the knowledge of mysteries opens the eyes of believers and sets them on a strong path of faith, the mystery of the Kingdom of God is a problem for those who are without faith and are outside of the salvational stream of the Messiah. In fact, rather than enlightening them, it blinds them and blunts their spiritual perception.

When such mysteries are given to those who are outside of Christ and to babies, the mystery of the Kingdom of God affects their hearing and makes them hear noise. The mystery of the Kingdom of God deforms their spiritual sensibilities and opens up wrong gates, or simply ends up dulling their understanding. According to Paul, the ministers of Christ are stewards and custodians of the mysteries of God in which they are required to be faithful. "Moreover it is required in stewards, that a man be found faithful" (1 Cor 4:1-2).

Even the speaking in tongues, which we exhibit in prayer, is called a mystery.

> ₂ For he that speaketh in an *unknown* tongue speaketh not unto men, but unto God: for no man understandeth *him*; howbeit in the spirit he speaketh mysteries. ₃ But he that prophesieth speaketh unto men *to* edification, and exhortation, and comfort. (1 Cor 14:2-3)

We are told that we should not be ignorant of the mystery regarding Israel's position in the present age and how it affects the salvation of the nations of the world.

> "For I would not, brethren, that ye should be ignorant of this mystery, lest ye should be wise in your own conceits; that blindness in part is happened to Israel, until the fullness of the Gentiles be come in". (Rom 11:25)

MYSTERIES ARE HIDDEN AND REVEALED BY GOD

Notice that one way to be established in the faith is by preaching Jesus Christ according to the revelation of the mystery which was kept hidden since the foundation of the world. The mystery is the sacrifice of Christ before the foundation of the world, which is activated for us in His death on the cross.

Paul says that this mystery of the Son of God is now made manifest by the Scriptures and of the prophets. Notice also, it does not say by "the Scriptures *and* the prophets" but "the Scriptures *of* the prophets." Since the New Testament had not been penned when Paul was writing it must then refer to the prophets of Israel which, at the time of the New Testament, were being read and understood through the lenses of the Holy Spirit as the direct command of the "everlasting God."

> " Notice that one way to be established in the faith is by preaching Jesus Christ according to the revelation of the mystery which was kept hidden since the foundation of the world.
> The mystery is the sacrifice of Christ before the foundation of the world, which is activated for us in His death on the cross. "

Paul said the Spirit of God reveals these mysteries to us. He refers to them as "the deep things of God" (1 Cor 2:10). Again, the tool for the unlocking of these mysteries by every nation on Earth is the "obedience of faith which comes through Jesus Christ." (Rom 1:5). It is according to the revelation of the mystery, which was kept secret since the world began, which is being revealed now, that we gain understanding of the power that is able to establish us in the faith.

25 Now to him that is of power to establish you according to my gospel, and the preaching of Jesus Christ, according to the revelation of the mystery, which was kept secret since the world began, 26 But now is made manifest, and by the Scriptures of the prophets,

according to the commandment of the everlasting God, made known to all nations for the obedience of faith: (Rom 16:25-26)

Paul says that the wisdom of God is spoken in a mystery that is hidden, ordained by God before the world. The idea that it is ordained before the world is itself a mystery that can only be searched out by the Spirit, who is the depth of God and the mystery of His being.

7 But we speak the wisdom of God in a mystery, *even* the hidden *wisdom,* which God ordained before the world unto our glory; 8 Which none of the princes of this world knew: for had they known *it,* they would not have crucified the Lord of glory. 9 But as it is written, Eye hath not seen, nor ear heard, neither have entered into the heart of man, the things which God hath prepared for them that love Him 10 But God hath revealed *them* unto us by his Spirit: for the Spirit searcheth all things, yea, the deep things of God. (1 Cor 2:7-10)

> **"** Only by the revelation of Jesus Christ through the Holy Spirit can we begin to grasp the meaning of these mysteries. Therefore, to argue that there are not mysteries today is to stand in direct opposition to the Scriptures, the prophets and even to the reality of the universe in which we live. **"**

In speaking of the transformation that will happen to those who bear the mark, who wake up from the sleepy slumber that has overtaken humankind and attain the resurrection of the Lord, He calls it a mystery. Everything in the text is couched in mystery. Being changed in a moment, in the twinkling of an eye, is a mystery. The transmutation of finite human DNA by the sound of the trumpet of the archangel, which moves it from corruption to incorruption, is a mystery. The transmutation of the human body from mortality to immortality is a mystery. 'Sin-iniquity' is a mystery, and so forth.

Only by the revelation of Jesus Christ through the Holy Spirit can we begin to grasp the meaning of these mysteries. Therefore, to argue that there are not mysteries today is to stand in direct opposition to the Scriptures, the prophets and even to the reality of the universe in which we live.

> [51] Behold, I shew you a mystery; we shall not all sleep, but we shall all be changed, [52] In a moment, in the twinkling of an eye, at the last trump: for the trumpet shall sound, and the dead shall be raised incorruptible, and we shall be changed. [53] For this corruptible must put on incorruption, and this mortal *must* put on immortality [54] So when this corruptible shall have put on incorruption, and this mortal shall have put on immortality, then shall be brought to pass the saying that is written, Death is swallowed up in victory [55] O death, where *is* thy sting? O grave, where *is* thy victory? [56] The sting of death *is* sin; and the strength of sin *is* the law. [57] But thanks *be* to God, which giveth us the victory through our Lord Jesus Christ. [58] Therefore, my beloved brethren, be ye stedfast, unmovable, always abounding in the work of the Lord, forasmuch as ye know that your labor is not in vain in the Lord. (1 Cor 15:51-58)

The gathering of all things in heaven and earth into the Kingdom of God through Christ is a mystery that God keeps in God's own hands until it is His good pleasure to make it known to His apostles and prophets. Everything mentioned in the passage above (I Cor. 15) is a mystery that cannot be explained except by revelation from the Spirit.

The fact that we shall not all sleep (physically die) but shall be changed - ἀλλαγησόμεθα - (1 Cor 15:51 ALF) from the Greek word *allasso* {al-las'-so} which means instant transmogrification, to exchange one mode of being for another, is mystery. The process of this transformation is a mystery because God alone knows the process. Resting passively in the future, it can only be perceived by a human being through the revelational insight that comes from the Spirit.

> 9 Having made known unto us the mystery of His will, according to His good pleasure which He hath purposed in Himself: 10 That in the dispensation of the fullness of times He might gather together in one all things in Christ, both which are in heaven, and which are on earth; *even* in Him: 11 In whom also we have obtained an inheritance, being predestinated according to the purpose of Him who worketh all things after the counsel of His own will: 12 That we should be to the praise of His glory, who first trusted in Christ. (Eph 1:9-12)

Again, Paul would have us understand that mysteries are only made known by revelation. Some people are given understanding of mysteries. There are mysteries that have not been made known to the sons of men in their natural existence but are revealed to "apostles and prophets by the Spirit." Paul says some mysteries have been made known to him by revelation and he prays that other believers may have the knowledge of the mystery of Christ.

> 3 How that by revelation He made known unto me the mystery; (as I wrote afore in few words, 4 Whereby, when ye read, ye may understand my knowledge in

the mystery of Christ) 5 Which in other ages was not made known unto the sons of men, as it is now revealed unto His holy apostles and prophets by the Spirit; 6 That the Gentiles should be fellow heirs, and of the same body, and partakers of His promise in Christ by the gospel. (Eph 3:3-6)

> **"** The gathering of all things in heaven and earth into the Kingdom of God through Christ is a mystery that God keeps in God's own hands until it is His good pleasure to make it known to His apostles and prophets. Everything mentioned in the passage above (I Cor. 15) is a mystery that cannot be explained except by revelation from the Spirit. **"**

In making known the mystery of marriage Paul says "This is a great mystery: but I speak concerning Christ and the church" (Eph 5:32). In fact, part of our prayer task should be for the apostles and prophets and yes, all members of the five-fold ministry - to open their mouth in boldness to make known the mystery of the Gospel.

As ambassadors of Christ to the world, our work is to make known the mystery of the gospel. The mystery of the gospel is greater than any mystery boasted of by the underworld or the occult. In fact, in one place Paul speaks of it as a threefold mystery: "the mystery of God, (the mystery) of the Father, and (the mystery) of Christ" (Col 2:2).

19 And for me, that utterance may be given unto me, that I may open my mouth boldly, to make known the mystery of the gospel, 20 For which I am an ambassador in bonds: that therein I may speak boldly, as I ought to speak. (Eph 6:19-20)

In the "acknowledgement of the mystery of God, and of the Father, and of Christ," we open ourselves to access all the other treasures of wisdom and knowledge in Christ. In this acknowledgement and access, the heart of the believer finds comfort. This causes us to be "knit together in love" and to come unto all the riches of the full assurance of understanding what God has for us. In other words, not acknowledging and accessing the mysteries impoverishes the church in many ways.

> **"** In the "acknowledgement of the mystery of God, and of the Father, and of Christ," we open ourselves to access all the other treasures of wisdom and knowledge in Christ. In this acknowledgement and access, the heart of the believer finds comfort. **"**

₂ that their hearts might be comforted, being knit together in love, and unto all riches of the full assurance of understanding, to the acknowledgement of the mystery of God, and of the Father, and of Christ; in whom are hid all the treasures of wisdom and knowledge. (Col 2:2 - 3)

THE MYSTERY OF INIQUITY

There is a mystery of iniquity which works in human beings. The breath of God's mouth or the direct flow of the essence of God into the context of that mystery is the only means to destroy it.

₇ For the mystery of iniquity doth already work: only He who now letteth *will let*, until he be taken out of the way. ₈ And then shall that Wicked be revealed, whom the Lord shall consume with the spirit of His mouth, and shall destroy with the brightness of His coming: 9 *Even him*, whose coming is after the working of Satan with all power and signs and lying wonders, 10 And with all deceivableness of unrighteousness in them that perish; because they received not the love of the truth, that they might be saved. 11 And for this cause God shall send them strong delusion, that they should believe a lie: 12 that they all might be damned who believed not the truth, but had pleasure in unrighteousness. (2 Th 2:7-12)

What we see now in the world is not the being referred to as "Wicked." We see the effects of the mystery of iniquity. That mystery itself is embedded in the personality called "Wicked." This mystery of iniquity has several aspects.

1. There is an essential, or being, aspect to this mystery of iniquity. The working of Satan is embedded in the intrinsic nature of the one in whom iniquity was first found and in whom all of its deadly mysteries are locked.

2. There is a three-part aspect to this mystery of iniquity- that of:

(a) power (b) signs (c) wonders, but all injected with lies.

3. There is the deceptiveness of unrighteousness in them that perish.

4. They received not the love of truth that they might be saved.

5. They have a delusional tendency leading to unbelief.

6. There is active belief in a lie.

7. There is hedonistic pleasure in unrighteousness

without repentance.

THE MYSTERY OF THE FAITH & THE MYSTERY OF GODLINESS

Furthermore, we are told that there is "the mystery of faith," which we are to hold in a pure conscience. Only those who hold this mystery of the faith should be considered for leadership within the church.

> $_9$ Holding the mystery of the faith in a pure conscience $_{10}$ And let these also first be proved; then let them use the office of Elder (1 Tim 3:9-10)

What is the mystery of faith that the elders should hold in a pure conscience? The answer to "the mystery of iniquity" that was discussed above is "the mystery of godliness." This mystery of Godliness is the person of the LORD Jesus Christ as expressed in the following passage from the Scriptures.

> $_{16}$ And without controversy great is the mystery of godliness: God was manifest in the flesh, justified in the Spirit, seen of angels, preached unto the Gentiles, believed on in the world, received up into glory. (1 Tim 3:16)

MYSTERY OF THE SEVEN CHURCHES

There are some mysteries, whose symbolism is made open, such as we find in John's description of the seven churches. However, their inner interrelations are not immediately shown. This means that though the mystery of the symbolism is manifest, the mystery of how they are actually interconnected and how they interact is not evident in the surface of the text. If the mysteries of their interrelationship and interactions were obvious there would not be so much controversy about them.

For example, are the seven angels of the churches pastors, apostles, prophets, evangelists or teachers? So the seven churches serve as a paradigm for the life of each church, congregation, and person who is the temple (church) of the LORD. To limit our understanding of these seven angels by saying that they are pastors is to ignore the other ascension gifts.

On the other hand, could they be an actual order of angels whose task it is to watch over the churches in a city or even a particular gathering of believers? Could the angels be archetypes of overseeing spiritual beings over the church? Could they be guardians of the divine glory that is present in the worshipping community of our Lord Jesus Christ?

Next, we know that the seven churches were actual churches which served as archetypal paradigms of what churches can become. They could also be seen from the perspective of multiplying 7 times 7, which is 49 - representing the church as the custodian of the blood that flowed through the stripes of the Lord Jesus Christ (The Church represents the birthing space of the jubilee of humanity - as 49 is the breaking into jubilee. It can also be seen as the movement from the bondage filled fallen creation into the new and free creation of the Messiah).

> The mystery of the seven stars which thou sawest in my right hand, and the seven golden candlesticks. The seven stars are the angels of the seven churches: and the seven candlesticks, which thou sawest, are the seven churches. (Rev 1:20)

There is also a time when the mysteries of God will end. Does this mean that God will cease being a mystery? The response will seem an obvious 'no'. However, the mysteries of God regarding all creation, the fall, redemption and all that pertains to it will be finished. God will never cease to be greater than the sum of all creation, hence always mysterious.

But in the days of the voice of the seventh angel, when he shall begin to sound, the mystery of God should be finished, as He hath declared to His servants the prophets. (Rev 10:7)

THE MYSTERY OF MYSTERY BABYLON

Another mystery in Scripture, which continues to stump preachers and scholars alike, is the mystery Babylon. In the book of Revelation, we see one of the seven angels that had the seven bowls, speaking with John the revelator saying, "Come hither, I will show thee the judgment of the great harlot."

This is a feminine principle capable of receiving seed from a plurality of sources and giving fruits to those who give her their seed, and in so doing maintains control of the sources and the recipients.

"That sits upon many waters," refers to this harlot controlling innumerable numbers of people by the covenants made with the kings of the earth who committed fornication. For generations these kings have given their seed to her and received her blood, spreading their connection to those that dwell on the earth. By this relationship many have been made drunken with the wine of her fornication - the religious network of idolatry and rebellion.

And he carried me away in the Spirit into a

wilderness: and I saw a woman sitting upon a scarlet-colored beast, full of names of blasphemy, having seven heads and ten horns. ₄ And the woman was arrayed in purple and scarlet, and decked with gold and precious stones and pearls, having in her hand a golden cup full of abominations, even the unclean things of her fornication, ₅ And upon her forehead *was* a name written, MYSTERY, BABYLON THE GREAT, THE MOTHER OF HARLOTS AND ABOMINATIONS OF THE EARTH. ₆ And I saw the woman drunken with the blood of the saints, and with the blood of the martyrs of Jesus: and when I saw her, I wondered with great admiration. (Rev 17:3-6)

It is so easy to equate this mystery to specific cities or empires in Europe. It should be remembered that it is not just Rome that drank the blood of saints, martyred the followers of Jesus Christ and other innocent men, women and children. There is the system of Cain and the residual influence of the reptilian seed, whose main purpose is to corrupt human DNA and make it non-salvageable.

Note also that the city was in the wilderness. The woman, of course, represents a city. This scarlet-colored beast will be a religious system whose main purpose is the blasphemy of God and His Messiah. The seven heads are related to governmental expressions of absolute authority in earthly governments. The ten horns are expressions of power, which have the capacity to bring the alchemical binary principles together on earth (the created sphere in general) and to create new things by which they think they have no need of the everlasting God.

This city is an antitype of the heavenly Jerusalem in that, whatever is in the New Jerusalem, this whorish city seeks to represent in a negative sense. It decks itself with gold, precious stones and pearls, but it feeds and lives from a cup full of abomination. Almost all of these cities, which serve as religious centers of the world, can be accused of embodying this "MYSTERY BABYLON." That is why it is a mystery. It cannot be grasped in one swoop.

But those who are wise watch for its manifestation, for it hides in the wilderness, sits upon the waters, and covers itself with religion and false spirituality - all the while focusing on abominating the Holy One. Now it could be Rome, Athens, Berlin, Abuja, Accra, Johannesburg, Beijing, Paris, St. Petersburg, Tokyo, London, Mecca, New Delhi and more. For the purpose is always to work against God and His Messiah.

According to the interpretation of the angel, this is not something to marvel about, for the beast has the ability to appear and disappear - "it was, and is not." Its place of ascent is out of the bottomless pit and its destination is perdition. Because of its glitter, bling and seeming depth of religious insight, the people of earth look upon her whenever she rises with great admiration. Those whose names were not written in the book of life from the foundation of the world are taken and deluded by the seeming pomp, glitter and power of the beast that appears and disappears, or seems to call things out of nothing - "was, and is not, and yet is".

THE SPIRIT, SOUL, MIND AND BODY

One reason that can be given for the movement away from the mystery of spiritual things and engagement with the supernatural is the Modern Western tendency to fragment these fundamentally interconnected worlds of spirit, soul and body. Of course, it often is necessary to postulate separation to study a particular part with greater precision. However, with complex organisms such as human beings, when one part is separated and studied it becomes like a shattered humpty-dumpty which cannot quite be put back together.

The whole universe is spiritual in that it moves and has its being in God - who is Spirit in the supreme sense of the word. Even fallen man (when considered in terms of soul, mind, and body) must be seen as an intrinsically interconnected organism. The body is not just matter, though in its present fallen state it is transitory and bound. Its origin and intrinsic nature is spiritual. The body came from God, who is Spirit (as the Lord Jesus Christ tells us in John 4:24). There is a dormant spiritual potential within it. The soul has that residue of spiritual effect from which it was created, even in its fall.

When the body becomes the true body of the Holy Spirit there is an activation of that dormant original spirituality by which it was formed. The soul's spiritual nature is shown in the fact that it came into being by the breath, wind-spirit of God. The vestiges of that original spirituality animate the mind of man.

They are interconnected. When we see the interconnectivity that is based on the original spiritual source of the three aspects of man, then even though we are fallen, we open up the way for experiencing super-sensuous or spiritual phenomenon. This may be one way to account for the "spiritual experiences" of so many people who have no relationship with God. The three dimensions of man are always in search of that original spiritual source, which is God. This can only be accomplished by being of the Spirit, through insertion into the life-giving blood of Jesus Christ.

THE HEART-MIND OF MAN

While the cerebral mind operates from the fallen nature of man (and in a sense operates from death and gives forth death even when it means the best) there is another mind which has long ceased to operate with any effectiveness in man. It has become deceitful, desperate, and wicked due to the fallenness of soul, body and natural mind. That is the 'heart-mind'.

The heart was the seat of the spirit before the fall of man. From there the mind of God operated to give man direct access to the thoughts and ways of God and helped man operate at the frequency of God. For only in and through the heart made alive by the life of God, set on fire by the Holy Spirit and enthroned by the Father can the 'heart-mind' be fully functional. That 'heart-mind' is where the mysteries of God and the universe are hidden.

The best way to access spiritual mysteries is to use the mind of your heart-mind, not just your rational-mind. Our heart-mind has greater capacity than we often realize. This heart-mind is able to remember large amounts of information and revelations. There is so much in our heart-mind memory - it is just that we have not been trained in how to unlock it.

The Bible says "He has made all things perfect in its way and has placed eternity in their hearts" (Eccl 3:12). The heart has revelation of eternal things - things that go back to the beginning of creation because the very principle of eternity is embedded in it by God at the moment of conception. One can even say that God has locked within the human heart the mystery of the universe.

One of the many reasons we are incapable of unlocking this resource of the heart-mind is because our whole life is filled with chatter coming from training, traditions, culture and experiences. Whenever the heart-mind attempts to grant us access into the eternal reserves within it, we get in the way of what is possible.

> **"** This is the mystery of God. Because only God can surround something and still get out of Himself and move above Himself. That is what makes God, God. Remember the heavens are inside of God, but God still rides on top of them. still rides over the heavens. **"**

One way to help unlock this eternity locked in the heart is to follow the biblical encouragement "Be still and know, that I AM God" (Psa 46:10). However, to unblock it we need the Spirit that put eternity there in the first place. The indwelling presence of the Holy Spirit is the key given to us so we may access this eternity placed within the heart.

The gateway into the universe is in the heart of man. It needs to be understood that to have this indwelling is to know the Messiah Jesus Christ. Our problem is that we often look at it the wrong way. We externalize eternity and internalize time. However, the indwelling of eternity and the indwelling of the Holy Spirit, as taught by Scripture, suggest that the problem of time and eternity is dealt with in the heart so that in our consciousness eternity is moved from being 'out there' to being 'in here' - within.

This confusion of eternity as being 'out there' is the source of the body/spirit confusion, in which the body is looked at as something completely removed from the spirit. Actually, the body should be looked at as an outflow of the spirit. As we grasp this indwelling eternity and its impact on the body, it changes our understanding of what is possible in the body. The body, rather than being a separate entity, is an extension of the spirit.

Therefore, as we begin examining the heavens, we must learn the protocol of reverence through prayer and deal with areas in our lives that might cause problems for us as we navigate the mystery of the heavens. As I have said, the first order of the protocol is acknowledging the Lordship of Jesus Christ, followed by an attentive listening to the Holy Spirit, while maintaining a meditative attitude and self-immersion in the Scriptures. Coming into the throne room of God through spiritual worship is also a protocol requirement.

Know also that in the heavens, you cannot introduce yourself to the Father on your own. Jesus must introduce you. "No one comes to the Father except by me." Jesus is saying you should not make any move unless the Spirit first directs you. Try to make sure you are standing firmly on the foundation of the blood of Jesus Christ.

As you begin this practice, do not try to figure out everything you will see in advance. This is a walk of faith, as is everything pertaining to our Christian walk. Sit in a quiet place, with your hands stretched half way open in front of you. Take a deep breath and exhale slowly. You may want to breathe in the first syllable of the name of Jesus "Jeeeee", then exhale with "suuuuus", inhale "Jeeeee", exhale suuuuus".

Do this as many times as you need to. Listen to the sound of the name of the LORD Jesus Christ as it vibrates through your body. Call upon His name until you feel His presence through the Holy Spirit. Proclaim the Lordship of Jesus Christ. Because you are not going to be able to do this on your own, make sure that Jesus is in the center of your space. Time and space cohere in him.

For Christo-centric meditations on the name of God with Dr O please go to www.seraphcreative.org/dro

THE STRUCTURE OF HEAVEN

HEAVEN IS IN GOD

Let's go through the Scriptures because it will help you to ground yourself. Psalm 57:5 says, "Be exalted, O God, above the heavens; Let Your glory be above all the earth." Now here is something you must understand. God is greater than the heavens. No matter how many heavens there are, remember that every heaven is nested in God. There is nothing outside of God.

The translations of Scripture always say "exalted." However, really the word should be "expanded." You are more expansive than the heavens. Because in Him we live, move and have our being. Everything is inside of God. We are going to deal with heaven and we're going to deal with hell. Why? Because hell is also inside of God - hell is not outside of God. You cannot have anything existing outside of God. Yes, even the devil moves, lives and is inside of God.

When the devil is cast down into the abyss, the abyss is in God Himself. There is no such thing as an abyss without God. Nothing exists outside of God. The world could not exist if God did not make a space for it to exist within Himself. So keep your mind from thinking that somewhere there is a heaven and you get to heaven and then God comes to meet you. God is more expansive than all the heavens - the structured heavens, the nested heavens, the heavens of the soul.

"Let Your glory be above all the earth." I'm trying not to get too preachy in terms of the Bible but you need this. You need these foundations so that, when we start talking about this revelations more, somebody won't write me and say, "Where is all of that in the Bible?"

Psalm 68:4 says, "Sing unto the Lord, sing praises to His name; Extol Him that rides upon the heavens, by His name Yah and rejoice before Him"

This is the mystery of God. Because only God can surround something and still get out of Himself and move above Himself. That is what makes God, God. Remember the heavens are inside of God, but God still rides on top of them. Because God's nature is different from your nature and mine, He is able to be in something and be outside of it at the same time. He is able to be fully present within and fully present outside.

You and I have not developed that ability; we have not come to that point yet. We are sons and daughters, but we have not been released to that yet. The heavens are in God, because their being is in God, but God still rides over the heavens.

"Extol Him that rides upon the heavens, By His name
Yah, and rejoice before Him." (Psa 68:4)

"A father of the fatherless, and a judge of the widow, is God in His holy habitation. God sets the solitary in families; then bringeth out those who are bound with chains; but the rebellious live in a dry land." (Psa 68: 5-6)

MOBILE, MALLEABLE AND SET HEAVENS

In Ezekiel and Daniel we see that there is a mobile throne" (or what might be considered a mobile heaven), there is a malleable heaven and there is a set heaven. We also find in Psalm 68:17 what might be interpreted as thrones of God which are mobile in nature "The chariots of God are twenty thousand, even thousands of angels: the Lord is among them, as in Sinai, in the holy place..." By mobile heaven I mean that which God rides and sets up sometimes to interact with His creatures. Since heaven is also where God is I consider that there is (are) a 'Mobile Heaven(s)'. Very few people can go to the mobile heaven, because in order to go to the mobile heaven, you have to be a person who moves in the glory. That is what God did in the wilderness, as seen in Exodus. Every time there was something that needed to "be", He moved. Anybody who did not move missed the movement. This heaven is only accessible by waters (as I explain later in this book).

2) There is a 'Malleable Heaven', which is a matrix type heaven that can be formed, reformed and pulled around based on your experience and what you need. God then joins you to create a particular heaven that fits into what you desire and into how He wants to meet your need. You're a child of God - and the Father builds a house according to the desires and needs of His child. The malleable heaven is accessible to anybody who has an intimate relationship with God. What happens is as you develop, God forms heaven and allows you to experience heaven in a form that is still developing. He forms it based on your experiences and what you need so that the more you mature, the more He opens it up and redesigns it - based on your desire and based on where you are going. He redesigns the heavens for you, so you can experience them.

3) Then there is the 'Set Heaven', which is a set position and where very few people can go to. In this heaven, we are talking

> **"** If we are co-laborers with God, it is not just to win souls and bring people to Jesus. **"**

about something that is already set in place. It is like a house that is set, and that is where most people cannot go. People who do go say, "Oh, I saw such wonderful things." God is ready for you to come there and, when you come, He knows what you enjoy and He makes it up so you can have fun. You and God make a heaven. You have to be at a certain level to be able to do that.

Remember, the Bible says we are co-laborers. If we are co-laborers with God, it is not just to win souls and bring people to Jesus. It's not just to tell people, "You know, Jesus loves you. I'm co-laboring with God to bring you into the Kingdom." You have nothing to do with people's salvation. If you are a co-heir and co-laborer, that is a very powerful thing. It is not at every level that you are a co-laborer with God. You have to grow up to a certain level for God to let you play with creating planets and creating heavens.

Most of the heavens that are created by the children of God, who are still growing in their maturity, are destroyed. It is because we are not ready to create a universe. You still contain within you the record of fallen DNA. Everything you create must be tried by fire. I Corinthians 3:12, "Every man's work must be tried by fire, whether if it be of gold, it shall abide; stone, [stubble], if it's wood it will burn. But the person will still be saved." You are not judged by God for creating a world that is not sustainable because you're not ready. It takes practice.

When the Bible talks about heaven it states things like

"God humbles Himself in order to look at the heavens." (Psa 113:6) How great must God be - to have to bow down to look at the heavens of the heavens of the heavens?

God has made Himself the playground for His children. Otherwise, you would have been gone. You would have been zapped, burned, crisped. He allows Himself to be a playground, just like your father. I'm sorry if you did not grow up with a father, but I still remember my father letting me jump all over him when I was a kid. I still remember my kids jumping all over me because I had become the playground for my children.

"Bless the Lord, all His works, in all places of His dominion. Bless the Lord, O my soul!" (Psa 103: 22)

All His works, everything in the universe has the capacity to be activated as spirit form. It is a hard thing for us as believers to believe. The universe is not as solid as you think it is. For example, silicon is sand. There is a lot of activities we can do with silicon in our computers - which are just sand. It conducts information and gives us things we would not have

> **"** All His works, everything in the universe has the capacity to be activated as spirit form. It is a hard thing for us as believers to believe. **"**

thought we could do. You need to understand this process. Even things in nature, when you understand and position yourself, can act for you.

What happened when Israel left Egypt? Flies. Hailstorm. Water. Flood. Everything can be activated to do what God wants it to do. Elements can be activated - they can become messengers of divinity. In every dimension of heaven there are elements - there are things there that can be activated in that dimension both for good and for bad, or for warfare - not for bad in the real world but for warfare and for peace.

When Moses is coming out of the land of Egypt with the Israelites, he parts the waters and they stand as a wall. Moses passes by, stretches his hand, and the waters fight, and Pharaoh's army died in the water.

> **"** In summary, when I think of heaven, biblically there are heavens of heavens of heavens. Secondly, I consider that the Kingdom of God includes all the heavens. **"**

Moses is talking to the people who are attacking him and he says "We shall see. God, do such and such to me if the earth does not open up its mouth right now and swallow them up". And guess what happened? The earth opened up... and they fell in.

So, there are the elements themselves. The very things you see at a certain level can be activated to be used. That is why God doesn't allow many people to have this kind of power. You should not seek this kind of power because you cannot handle it. You hear God talking about witchcraft and condemning it mainly because there are principles and laws in nature - when you get to a certain place you can actually activate these principles and use it to hurt people. Because your nature, the monster DNA in you, is not going to let you use it just for good. Very few people receive this power and remain the same. So, be careful what you look for.

Then Psalm 103 says "Bless the Lord, O my soul! and all that is within me". This includes your body, however the soul is the final level of the messenger principle that God sends in every dimension.

In summary, when I think of heaven, biblically there are

heavens of heavens of heavens. Secondly, I consider that the Kingdom of God includes all the heavens. The heavens include the planets and everything else you can think of - 100 billion galaxies all are part of the heavens. So if one were sitting in a galaxy ten billion light years away, the earth would be a dimension of the heavens.

ISRAEL AS A PATTERN OF HEAVEN

All of Israel's religious activities were patterns of things in heaven. The sacrifices were done so that through all of the feasts, rituals, garments, gates of the temple and city and the structures of the heavenlies could be clearly envisioned and followed until the heavenly things were purified by the better sacrifice. The heavenly man (the archetypal Man) came and restored the pattern of man to its heavenly measurement by the person of the LORD's Messiah - The Man Christ Jesus. The sacrifice of the LORD Jesus Christ was to make tainted dimensions of the heavens pure again, to open its gateways and pathways and to purify us so that we can again navigate the heavens as washed beings. The fathers in Scripture desired to enter the heavenlies but could only look from afar. Their desire connected them to God in such a way that He was "not ashamed to be called their God: for he hath prepared for them a city" (Heb 11:16).

> **"** All of Israel's religious activities were patterns of things in heaven. **"**

[23] *It was* therefore necessary that the patterns of things in the heavens should be purified with these; but the heavenly things themselves with better sacrifices than these. (Heb 9:23).

> **"** Those patterns were all shadows of heavenly things that could be seen dimly and from afar. However, we who are the heirs of the manifest Messiah are able now through His shed blood to enter boldly into the heavenlies - in fact into the throne. **"**

Those patterns were all shadows of heavenly things that could be seen dimly and from afar. However, we who are the heirs of the manifest Messiah are able now through His shed blood to enter boldly into the heavenlies - in fact into the throne.

₅ Who serve unto the example and shadow of heavenly things, as Moses was admonished of God when he was about to make the tabernacle: for, see, saith he, *that* thou make all things according to the pattern shewed to thee in the mount.

₆ But now hath he obtained a more excellent ministry, by how much also he is the mediator of a better covenant, which was established upon better promises. (Heb 8:5-6)

Since Israel is the earthly pattern of the heavenly reality according to the above Scripture, we can begin to look at the structures of heaven by looking at how God organized and arranged the tribes of Israel in the wilderness. All their encampments were to face the center of where the tabernacle was situated according to Numbers 2:2.

₂ Every man of the children of Israel shall pitch by his own standard, with the ensign of their father's house: far off facing the tabernacle of the congregation shall they pitch.

~3~ And on the east side toward the rising of the sun shall they of the standard of the camp of Judah pitch throughout their armies: and Nahshon the son of Amminadab *shall be* captain of the children of Judah.

~4~ And his host, and those that were numbered of them, *were* threescore and fourteen thousand and six hundred.

~5~ And those that do pitch next unto him *shall be* the tribe of Issachar: and Nethaneel the son of Zuar *shall be* captain of the children of Issachar.

~6~ And his host, and those that were numbered thereof, *were* fifty and four thousand and four hundred.

~7~ *Then* the tribe of Zebulun: and Eliab the son of Helon *shall be* captain of the children of Zebulun.

~8~ And his host, and those that were numbered thereof, *were* fifty and seven thousand and four hundred.

~9~ All that were numbered in the camp of Judah *were* a hundred thousand and fourscore thousand and six thousand and four hundred, throughout their armies. These shall first set forth. (Num 2:4-9)

THE SECOND SET OF THE ENCAMPMENT WAS TO THE SOUTH, HEADED BY THE TRIBE OF RUBEN:

~10~ "On the south side *shall be* the standard of the camp of Reuben by their armies, and the leader of the sons of Reuben: Elizur the son of Shedeur,

~11~ and his army, even their numbered men, 46,500.

12 "And those who camp next to him *shall be* the tribe of Simeon, and the leader of the sons of Simeon: Shelumiel the son of Zurishaddai,

13 and his army, even their numbered men, 59,300.

14 "Then *comes* the tribe of Gad, and the leader of the sons of Gad: Eliasaph the son of Deuel,

15 and his army, even their numbered men, 45,650.

16 "The total of the numbered men of the camp of Reuben: 151,450 by their armies. And they shall set out second. (Num 2:10-16 NAS)

TO THE WEST WAS THE CAMP OF THE TRIBE OF EPHRAIM:

18 "On the west side *shall be* the standard of the camp of Ephraim by their armies, and the leader of the sons of Ephraim *shall be* Elishama the son of Ammihud,

19 and his army, even their numbered men, 40,500.

20 "And next to him *shall be* the tribe of Manasseh, and the leader of the sons of Manasseh: Gamaliel the son of Pedahzur,

21 and his army, even their numbered men, 32,200.

22 "Then *comes* the tribe of Benjamin, and the leader of the sons of Benjamin: Abidan the son of Gideoni,

23 and his army, even their numbered men, 35,400.

[24] "The total of the numbered men of the camp of Ephraim: 108,100, by their armies. And they shall set out third. (Num 2:18-24 NAS)

TO THE NORTH WAS THE TRIBE OF DAN:

[25] "On the north side *shall be* the standard of the camp of Dan by their armies, and the leader of the sons of Dan: Ahiezer the son of Ammishaddai,

[26] and his army, even their numbered men, 62,700.

[27] "And those who camp next to him *shall be* the tribe of Asher, and the leader of the sons of Asher: Pagiel the son of Ochran,

[28] and his army, even their numbered men, 41,500.

[29] "Then *comes* the tribe of Naphtali, and the leader of the sons of Naphtali: Ahira the son of Enan,

[30] and his army, even their numbered men, 53,400.

[31] "The total of the numbered men of the camp of Dan, was 157,600. They shall set out last by their standards." (Num 2:25-31 NAS)

THE ENCAMPMENT OF THE OLD SYSTEM OF NUMBERS CHAPTER 2

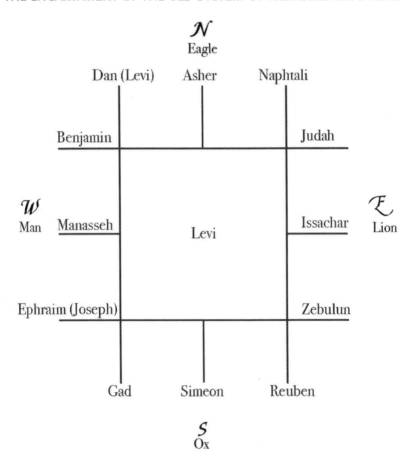

THE ENCAMPMENT OF THE NEW SYSTEM OF REVELATION

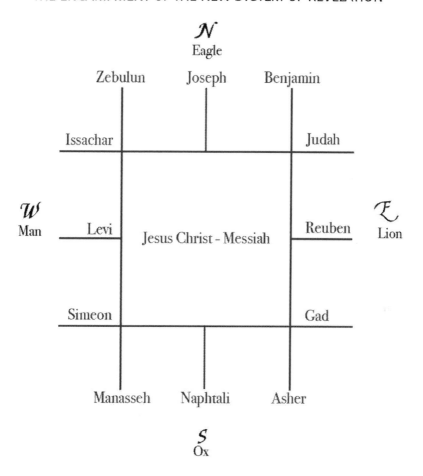

HASHAMAYIM & THE NATURE
OF HEAVEN

Since this book is on the structures of heaven and the angelic we will begin by looking at the meaning of heaven. We are going to deal with these things based on Scripture.

The Bible begins with the creation of the heavens: "In the beginning God created the heavens and the earth" (Genesis 1:1) and ends with a description of the heavens and the earth in the new aeon in Revelation chapters 21 and 22. Scripture returns repeatedly to the idea of the heavens using various metaphors, paradigms, and types. These representations point us toward an understanding of the structures of heaven. They also teach us how things operate within them.

We always want to ground what we do on Scripture. We can speculate, we can interpret and do all kinds of exercises but it always has to be grounded on Scripture. We cannot avoid going back to Scripture. In this present age we have a tendency as human beings to wander off but the Scriptures ground us and protect us. The Bible says that the Word of God is a living thing and life giving in its very nature. It alone serves as our protection. That is why we need to focus on it.

First, we want to begin by defining scripturally what heaven is. The Hebrew word for heaven is 'HaShamayim'. The word always occurs in plural from, so it should be translated

> **"** First, we want to begin by defining scripturally what heaven is. The Hebrew word for heaven is 'HaShamayim'. **"**

'the heavens' or 'the heavenlies'. (Some Hebrew scholars say it is a "double singular.") This is a silly way of saying that there is only one heaven. We are speaking about more than one heaven connected to a single source. Inherent in the language is a plural perspective of the heavens.

The Scriptures in the original language seldom uses singular to refer to the heavens, except maybe when it is translated in English. However, in the Hebrew, it is always in the plural - 'the heavens'. Maybe one can argue that in one or two places, such as in the Lord's Prayer, there is a "heaven" that is just a single location but that is in NT Greek οὐρανός "oo-ran-os". However, there are places where the Greek plural "oo-ran-ois" is used which will be a direct translation of the Hebrew word "HaShamayim". The translation from the Aramaic/Hebrew to Greek maintains this idea of plural heavens found in the Hebrew. This plurality of heavens is stated several times in the baptismal narrative found in the synoptic gospels. "After being baptized, Jesus came up immediately from the water; and behold, *the heavens* were opened, and he saw the Spirit of God descending as a dove *and* lighting on Him" (Mat 3:16), and further in Matthew 17 "and behold, *a voice out of the heavens* said, "This is My beloved Son, in whom I am well-pleased." Here we note that the voice of God, in its plural majesty, comes not on a one dimensional or from a one sphere heaven but comes simultaneously from all the dimensions and soars simultaneously - as God himself is everywhere. To that effect we read, "... and behold, a voice out of the heavens said, "This is My beloved Son, in whom I am well-pleased." (see also Mark 1:10-11).

Furthermore, when speaking of the end of any age, Jesus says it is followed by tribulations, the darkening of the sun and the moon, the falling of the stars from the sky of the particular world whose age is coming to a close and then to end it he says "men fainting from fear and the expectation of the things which are coming upon the world; for the powers of the *heavens* will be shaken." (Luke 21:26 NAS, see also Matt 24:29 and Mark 13:25)

Again when speaking of the transaction of heaven into any circumstance, person, atmosphere of epoch and especially as relating to himself as the Son of Man, Jesus says, "you will see *the heavens opened* and the angels of God ascending and descending on the Son of Man." (John 1:5) But the idea of plural heavens in the New Testament is not stated merely as a theory as we are told that when Stephen operates under the vision of his martyrdom in Acts 7:56 that "he said, 'Behold, *I see the heavens opened* up and the Son of Man standing at the right hand of God'," thus also stating that it is possible for a believer to see in one sweeping moment the plural heavens.

Further, when speaking as to the ascension of the Lord Jesus Christ in Ephesians 4:10, we are told that the ascension of Jesus Christ is not just an ascent into heaven, singular, but an ascent far above the heavens, plural. "He *who descended is Himself also He who ascended far above all the heavens*, so that He might fill all things." So we can conclude that in the Scriptures the Hebrew is always HaShamayim (plural) and in many cases in the Greek the plural ou-ran-ois is used also. Why then would anyone want to argue that there is only one heaven? Such arguments are the reason for the confusion that has plagued our generation of Christians.

Why did Paul say, "I was caught up to the third heaven"? Since the Bible speaks of plural heavens and Paul says he was caught up to the third heaven in the book of Corinthians, it is better to take the word of the Bible than the words of theologians in this case.

> **"** The patterns of Israel's religion represent different heavenly dimensions. There are 'nested ecologies of heavens' within God in that they sit next to one another, joined, interrelated and yet are separate. **"**

The Scriptures even speak of "the heaven of the heavens."

> "Behold, the heaven and the heaven of *heavens* is the LORD'S thy God, the earth *also*, with all that therein *is.*" (Deut 10:14)

> But will God indeed dwell on the earth? "Behold, the heaven and heaven of heavens cannot contain thee; how much less this house that I have builded?" (1 Kings 8:27).

In the Scriptures we are actually dealing with structures of heaven. We are dealing with varieties and levels of heavens. I do not really like using the word "level," because "level" makes it seem like one is dealing with vertical or even horizontal linearity. One can use the term "level" as long as it is remembered that such language can actually short-circuit certain spiritual movements. Therefore, I prefer the word "dimensions" of heavens.

The patterns of Israel's religion represent different heavenly dimensions. There are 'nested ecologies of heavens' within God in that they sit next to one another, joined, interrelated and yet are separate.

Twelve dimensions of this are revealed for us in the Old Testament in the formation of the tribes of Israel, their interplay in the ritual settings in the wilderness and even in the sharing of the Land of Israel.

Job speaks of God being in the heights of heaven and that God walks in the circuits of heaven, implying that there are sequences of progressive passages or pathways in the heavens (Job 22:12-14).

In Solomon's prayer (1 Kings 8:22-53) there are fifteen mentions of heaven and thirteen of the mentioned heavens come from the lips of Solomon. These thirteen mentions are representations of Israel in her thirteen families, which are the shadow of the heavenlies. There are two other references to heaven within the context of the prayer, making them a total of fifteen. The two represent the upper and the lower heavens, or the City of God and the city of man. The passage begins with the statement that "Solomon … spread forth his hands towards heaven."

₂₂ And Solomon stood before the altar of the LORD in the presence of all the congregation of Israel, and spread forth his hands toward heaven: (2 Kings 8:22)

The spreading of the two hands speaks symbolically of the upper and the lower heavens. The second mention of heaven is actually the highest heaven that the psalmist refers to - the heaven to which David was raised. It is the heaven above, where the supreme throne of God is established, from whence all thrones derive their authority.

In the language of the Bible this heaven is directly connected to the earth. God has a special interest in the earth given the fact that only here on earth does there exists a record of God's life and spirit in the form of a human being which can be transferred to other dimensions.

Here the seat of covenant of the heart abides, and the mercy seat shines. This dimension is where the psalmist says:

"The LORD *is* in his holy temple, the LORD'S throne *is* in heaven: his eyes behold, his eyelids try, the children of men" (Psa 11:4).

Here, in this dimension of heaven, is where the temple of heaven is and where the ark in heaven is kept, as we read in Revelation 11:19.

"And the temple of God was opened in heaven, and there was seen in his temple the ark of his testament: and there were lightnings, and voices, and thunderings, and an earthquake, and great hail." (Rev 11:19)

The lightnings and the thunders indicate the going forth of the creations emanating from the throne of God. From this heaven wars are made for the people of God.

> **"** It is the desire of the Father that we know the answer to such questions and thereby function according to the ordinances of heaven. In fact, it is in knowing these ordinances that we can set up the dominion given to us on the earth. **"**

11 And it came to pass, as they fled from before Israel, *and* were in the going down to Bethhoron, that the LORD cast down great stones from heaven upon them unto Azekah, and they died: *they were* more which died

with hailstones than *they* whom the children of Israel slew with the sword. (Jos 10:11)

Deborah tells us, "They fought from heaven" (Jdg 5: 20-21) and then explains that the stars in their movements around the heavens fought against Sisera.

$_{20}$ They fought from heaven; the stars in their courses fought against Sisera. $_{20}$ The river of Kishon swept them away, that ancient river, the river Kishon. O my soul, thou has trodden down strength. (Jdg 5:20-21)

The movement of the stars in heaven affected the flow of the river of Kishon, which then swept the armies of Sisera away. She calls the river "that ancient river." This "ancient river" is not a reference to the stream that runs through Palestine.

The river Kishon, according to Jewish sources, was in the piece of land assigned to the tribe of Issachar, which was then allotted

> **"** Notice how many times in the beginning of the prayer of Solomon the name of David is repeated as it relates to this mention of heaven. **"**

to the Gershonites of the tribe of Levi. The Gershonites were descendants of Moses, the Man of God. This could be a reference to the power which God gave Moses over water (Jdg 5:20-21).

In 1 Samuel, we are told that:

"The adversaries of the LORD shall be broken to pieces; (because) out of heaven shall He thunder upon them: the LORD shall judge the ends of the earth; and He shall give strength unto his king, and exalt the horn of his anointed (1 Sa 2:10).

In the Bible, the heavens are said to have foundations thus again saying that we can speak of multiple heavens.

"Then the earth shook and trembled; the foundations of heaven moved and shook, because He was wroth" (Psalm 18:7).

When people's sins are made manifest, the heavens act to reveal them. "The heavens shall reveal his iniquity; and the earth shall rise up against him" (Job 20:27). The pillars of heaven that tremble and are astonished at the reproof of the Lord are not stone pillars but living beings carrying the divine majesty of righteousness and mercy.

When we speak of the structures of the heavens we are not merely trying to divide that which God has not divided. There is the dividing of the sea by God's power and understanding, along with the passage in the creation story where we read of "waters" and "let it divide the waters from the water."

"And God made the firmament, and divided the waters which *were* under the firmament from the waters which *were* above the firmament: and it was so. 8 And God called the firmament Heaven. And the evening and the morning were the second day" (Gen 1:6-8).

Job 26:11-13 indicates that God himself structured the heavens in multiplicity. In the book of Job there is a curious passage. Elohim

> **"** When we speak of the structures of the heavens we are not merely trying to divide that which God has not divided. There is the dividing of the sea by God's power and understanding, along with the passage in the creation story where we read of "waters" and "let it divide the waters from the water." **"**

is said to garnish the heavens with His Spirit or the Wind. This is immediately followed with the idea that God formed the crooked serpent. It seems that this is not a reference to an ordinary serpent but to a supernatural concept. "By his spirit he hath garnished the heavens; his hand hath formed the crooked serpent" (Job 26:11-13).

It is the desire of the Father that we know the answer to such questions and thereby function according to the ordinances of heaven. In fact, it is in knowing these ordinances that we can set up the dominion given to us on the earth. When we operate as people seated in the heavenly places, in the power of God before whose throne we dwell, we may lift up our voice to the clouds in His name so that an abundance of waters may cover us and the world.

This abundance of waters refers to the glory of the LORD out of the heavens. By the same connection to the heavens to which we have access through the blood of Jesus Christ we can call forth lightning, which are flashes of the presence of the Shekinah, and they will show up in various places and all flesh will see His glory.

Wisdom, as we know, is a gift from heaven, for James tells us to ask of God who gives wisdom. The book of Job asks,

"Who hath put wisdom in the inward parts? Or who hath given understanding to the heart? $_{37}$ Who can number the clouds in wisdom? Or who can stay the bottles of heaven?" (Job 38:33-37)

Notice how many times in the beginning of the prayer of Solomon the name of David is repeated as it relates to this mention of heaven.

₂₃ And he said, LORD God of Israel, *there is* no God like thee, in heaven above, or on earth beneath, who keepest covenant and mercy with thy servants that walk before thee with all their heart; ₂₄ Who hast kept with thy servant David my father that thou promisedst him; thou spakest also with thy mouth, and hast fulfilled *it* with thine hand, as it is this day. ₂₅ Therefore, now LORD God of Israel, keep with thy servant David my father that thou promisedst him, saying, There shall not fail thee a man in my sight to sit on the throne of Israel; so that thy children take heed to their way, that they walk before me as thou hast walked before me." (1 Kings 8:23-25)

Solomon speaks of the heaven above, where covenants are kept and mercy flows, connected with the hearts of the holy ones. Here the God of David, the keeper of promises, speaks directly to the one who sits on the throne of Israel as long as his walk reflects directly what is done in the throne room of God.

When Moses prays for God to look down from heaven, the reference is to this dimension:

₂₆ "Look down from thy holy habitation, from heaven, and bless thy people Israel, and the land which thou hast given us, as thou swarest unto our fathers, a land that floweth with milk and honey" (Deut 26:15).

In this dimension of heaven, verification of the fulfilled promises are made and laid at the feet of the Master of the universe.

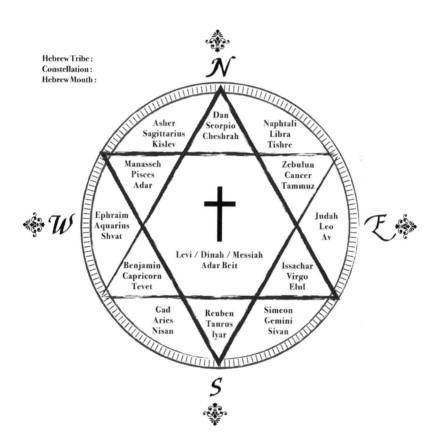

THE TRIBE AND THE CONSTELLATION

At a certain point in his prayer, Solomon uses a Hebraism of a combination of three heavens as he says, "heaven, the heaven, and the heaven of heavens cannot contain God." How much less the temple he had just built.

> $_{27}$ But will God indeed dwell on the earth? Behold, *the heaven* and *heaven of heavens* cannot contain thee; how much less this house that I have builded?" (1 Kings 8:27)

> $_{30}$ "And hearken thou to the supplication of thy servant....and hear thou in *heaven* thy dwelling place; and when thou hearest, forgive. (1 Kings 8:30)

The first dimension deals with the highest throne of God. The mention of the three heavens (which seems to cause confusion and to be the basis of Paul's vision of being caught into the third heaven) is a concentric representation of the twelve tribes of Israel. They are mentioned again in the book of Revelation where reference is made to how Israel was divided in the wilderness around the tabernacle.

Within each of the four dimensions are three tribes of Israel, representing four dimensions in three spheres, which equals both seven and twelve - which then means that Israel, in her configuration, represented both the Sabbath (7) and the star systems (12) as well.

HEAVENLY ADMINISTRATIONS

Though Solomon does not mention the constellations, it does appear to be the idea behind mentioning heaven 13 times – the top most heaven, where the word "above" occurs, being the matrix from which all are birthed. From heaven the dwelling place of God, the LORD God hears prayers, supplications, and the cries of his servants. For there, only "this day abides."

30 And hearken thou to the supplication of thy servant, and of thy people Israel, when they shall pray toward this place: and hear thou in heaven, thy dwelling place, and when thou hearest, forgive. 32 Then hear thou in heaven and do, and judge thy servants..."

From heaven, men's trespasses against their neighbors ascend and are heard, judged and arbitrated. Only in heaven is justification to righteousness obtained. In heaven, strategies for warfare and victory are obtained.

34 Then hear thou in heaven and forgive the sin of thy people Israel, and bring them again unto the land which thou gavest unto their fathers. 35 When heaven is shut up and there is no rain..."

When heaven is shut up, and there is no rain, it can be unlocked and rain can be released. The rain of blessings, abundance, prosperity, and health can only be released from heaven.

36 "Then hear thou in heaven, and forgive the sin of thy servants, and of thy people Israel, that thou teach them the good way wherein they should walk, and give rain upon thy land, which thou hast given to thy people for an inheritance."

37 If there be in the land famine, if there be pestilence, blasting, mildew, locust, or if there be caterpillar; if their enemy besiege them in the land of their cities; whatsoever plague, whatsoever sickness *there be*;

38 What prayer and supplication soever be *made* by any man, *or* by all thy people Israel, which shall know every man the plague of his own heart, and spread forth his hands toward this house:

39 "Then hear thou in heaven thy dwelling place, (provisions) and forgive, and do, and give to every man according to his ways, whose heart thou knowest; (for thou, *even* thou only, knowest the hearts of all the children of men ;)

40 That they may fear thee all the days that they live in the land which thou gavest unto our fathers.

41 Moreover concerning a stranger, that *is* not of thy people Israel, but cometh out of a far country for thy name's sake;

42 (For they shall hear of thy great name, and of thy strong hand, and of thy stretched out arm ;) when he shall come and pray toward this house;

43 Hear thou in heaven thy dwelling place, (judgment and mercy for the nations) and do according to all that the stranger calleth to thee for: that all people of the earth may know thy name, to fear thee, as *do* thy people Israel; and that they may know that this house, which I have builded, is called by thy name.

₄₄ If thy people go out to battle against their enemy, whithersoever thou shalt send them, and shall pray unto the LORD toward the city which thou hast chosen, and *toward* the house that I have built for thy name:

₄₅ Then hear thou in heaven their prayer and their supplication, and maintain their cause.

₄₆ If they sin against thee, (for *there* is no man that sinneth not,) and thou be angry with them, and deliver them to the enemy, so that they carry them away captives unto the land of the enemy, far or near;

₄₇ *Yet* if they shall bethink themselves in the land whither they were carried captives, and repent, and make supplication unto thee in the land of them that carried them captives, saying, We have sinned, and have done perversely, we have committed wickedness;

₄₈ And *so* return unto thee with all their heart, and with all their soul, in the land of their enemies, which led them away captive, and pray unto thee toward their land, which thou gavest unto their fathers, the city which thou hast chosen, and the house which I have built for thy name:

₄₉ Then hear thou their prayer and their supplication in heaven thy dwelling place, and maintain their cause,

₅₀ And forgive thy people that have sinned against thee, and all their transgressions wherein they have transgressed against thee, and give them compassion before them who carried them captive, that they may have compassion on them:

~51~ For they *be* thy people, and thine inheritance, which thou broughtest forth out of Egypt, from the midst of the furnace of iron: ~52~ That thine eyes may be open unto the supplication of thy servant, and unto the supplication of thy people Israel, to hearken unto them in all that they call for unto thee.

~53~ For thou didst separate them from among all the people of the earth, *to be* thine inheritance, as thou spakest by the hand of Moses thy servant, when thou broughtest our fathers out of Egypt, O Lord GOD.

~54~ And it was *so*, that when Solomon had made an end of praying all this prayer and supplication unto the LORD, he arose from before the altar of the LORD, from kneeling on his knees with his hands spread up to heaven." (1 Ki 8:22-54)

DIFFERENT FREQUENCIES OF HEAVEN

The various spheres of heaven represent not just different vibrational frequencies but a variety of spiritual eco-waves that affect human beings and all of creation. For each new dimension of heaven entered into, sound frequencies and spiritual eco-waves are released, as something new is created. While there are not clearly disclosed and exact structures of the Heavens there are paradigmatic hints and pointers showing insight into the structures of Heaven in various passages of Scripture.

Since the Word created everything in the world we may

use the terms 'vibrations' and 'frequencies' to indicate impacts and effects of the various dimensions of these structures as indicated in Scripture. Another point to keep in mind is that all things in the world have an interwoven spiritual fabric.

We are not talking about structures mainly in terms of their physical expression or solidity, which is not malleable. The use of the term *vibration* almost suggests that the heavens are a living organism. Even living organisms have structures. Since we teach that the human soul, spirit and ultimately the redeemed body will dwell in some form of heaven, whether it be in hyper-space or in heaven that has come to earth, its spirituality is fundamental because heaven was formed within and exists in God, who is Spirit.

THE THRONES OF THE HEAVENS

"The Lord has prepared His throne in the heavens;
and his kingdom ruleth over all" (Psa 103:19-22)

The psalmist tells us that all dimensions in the heavenlies find their ultimate expression in the throne of God, from which every other throne derives its existence and authority. In the heavens is where the ultimate throne of God is. It is where everything starts and everything finds its end.

There is a need to understand that as planets are nested within various places in space, so there are nested heavens within God. These heavens all have thrones that serve as God's seat of rest. From these thrones God's representatives direct that particular dimension. In every heaven or heavenly dimension there is a throne.

Furthermore, if the idea of Plurality of heaven is accurate, then the Throne (singular) of God sits above all other thrones, far above all the heavens. From this Ultimate Throne emerge all other thrones. In every dimension there exists God's Throne - God's place of restful authority. Every being, in every dimension, must deal with the fact that God's "Kingdom ruleth over all." The throne of the Lord serves as "the foundations of heaven" (2 Sam 22:8).

[19] "The LORD hath prepared His throne in the

heaven and His kingdom ruleth over all. 20 Bless the LORD, ye His angels that excel in strength, that do His commandments, hearkening unto the voice of His Word. 21 Bless ye the LORD all His hosts, ye ministers of His, that do His pleasure. 22 Bless the LORD, all His works in all places of His dominion: bless the LORD, O my soul." (Psa 103:19-22)

Angels, hosts, ministers, His works and souls are found within every nested heaven in order for that dimension to be complete. The only thing that is missing in most of these heavenly dimensions is man's soul. So the redemption of the soul of man is meant to complete every dimension of heaven and to put in place the final throne for God to rest His authority over all creation. It is to this throne of God that Jeremiah refers when he says, "A glorious high throne from the beginning is the place of our sanctuary" (Jer 17:12).

According to the Scriptures, there is a dimension where the ultimate throne of God is. This dimension is above the heavens. For example, we read from Moses that:

26 "There is none like the God of Jeshurun, *Who rides the heavens* to your help, And through the skies in His majesty. 27 "The eternal God is a dwelling place, And underneath are the everlasting arms; And He drove out the enemy from before you, And said, 'Destroy!' (Deut 33:26-27)

This is the place of eternity from which the Eternal God, who is the refuge of His people, rides.

> **"** There is a need to understand that as planets are nested within various places in space, so there are nested heavens within God. These heavens all have thrones that serve as God's seat of rest. **"**

From this eternal place God reaches down His everlasting arms and places them underneath His people's arms and uses them to thrust out the enemy from before them, saying to His people "Destroy."

The heavens themselves are the throne of God because God sits over the heavens. It is not just that the earth is directly connected to the heavens where God comes to rest His feet but that the earth itself, and specifically Jerusalem, is the throne of the God-man, the Messiah. The idea of rest is vital here because it could mean that the earth is of direct interest to God and serves as the place of God's manifest workings.

It can also refer to man as the dwelling place of God. Therefore the earth, as the abode of humanity, now comes to serve as God's resting place. In a sense, man is the final extension of the divine being and the place of God coming to rest.

In Isaiah, the LORD says:

"Thus saith the LORD, The heaven *is* my throne, and the earth *is* my footstool: where *is* the house that ye build unto me? and where *is* the place of my rest?" (Isa 66:1-2).

Of all the things that God has made, it is man whom God looks to as His divine resting place. Man is then the throne of God on the earth.

THE THRONE OF GOD IS HIDDEN FROM MAN

The Throne of God is held back from human beings by a

cloud. This is why I believe the Bible states so often about how Moses went into the cloud. According to the passage in Job, God holds back the face of His seat of honor or "throne" הָסְכֹ־יְנָפּ זָחָאָמ (Job 26:9 WTT). The idea here is that this throne is God's personal possession which He encloses *(machatz)* by spreading His cloud upon it (Job 26:9).

Could the veil in the temple that divided the holy place from the Holy of Holies have signified this holding back of the face of the throne by the spreading of clouds to keep it from any intrusive gaze of the profane? The answer is obviously yes. This throne of God is not a temporary throne but a throne that is forever and ever. It is based on the eternity of God's own throne that God promises David, "Thy seed will I establish forever, and build up thy throne to all generations. Selah" (Psa 89:4).

₁ "In the year that king Uzziah died I saw also the Lord sitting upon a throne, high and lifted up, and his train filled the temple. ₂ Above it stood the seraphim: each one had six wings; with twain he covered his face, and with twain he covered his feet, and with twain he did fly. ₃ And one cried unto another, and said, Holy, holy, holy, *is* the LORD of hosts: the whole earth *is* full of his glory. ₄ And the posts of the door moved at the voice of him that cried, and the house was filled with smoke." (Isa 6:1-4)

The Scriptures give the understanding that there is more than one throne. We see intimation of this in the thrones that Solomon built in his throne room, the description of the throne room of God, and the dimensions of the city of God as described by John in the book of Revelation (Rev 4:1-4).

₄ Around the throne were twenty - four thrones; and upon the thrones I saw twenty - four elders sitting, clothed in white garments, and golden crowns on their heads (Rev 4:4 ASV).

THE THRONE OF GOD AND JUDGING

The throne of God is where God sits, judging what is right and maintaining the right cause of His servants. From the throne that sits above the waters and the heavens the nations are rebuked and the wicked are destroyed. This is the only place where the name of a person or a nation can be wiped out forever and ever. Here is where the enemy's destructions come to a permanent end and where cities and nations fall and come into ruin. This is the place where the verdict is pronounced, "Destroyed." Here the memorial of Babylon was judged and sentenced to be perished forever.

The destruction of a memorial does not mean that a generation will not remember the nation or the city, but that the very seed of the city will never be allowed to sprout again because its record is wiped out from the books of heaven. That this throne is a throne of Judgment is supported by various places in Scripture. "But the LORD shall endure forever: He hath prepared His throne for judgment" (Psa 9:4-7). Part of the reason for the building of God's throne is to execute judgment.

THE EYES OF THE THRONE

The throne of God is filled with eyes. As the LORD enters His holy temple and sits on the LORD'S throne in heaven, these eyes begin to move in every direction and their piercing gazes try the children of men (Psa 11:4). We know from the Revelation of the LORD Jesus to John that there is a sea before the throne that is so calm it looks like glass or crystal. Even that sea of glass seems to describe the seeing capacity of the throne and the One who sits upon it.

The seer, who is John, then tells us that "in the midst of the throne, and round about the throne, were four beasts full of eyes before and behind" (Rev 4:6). Later on John tells us that these living creatures that were like a lion, a calf, a man and a flying eagle which were "full of eyes within" and they rest not day and night saying, "Holy, holy, holy, Lord God Almighty, which was, and is, and is to come" (Rev 4:6-8). It is not just that God sees all but even His throne is built as a seeing chamber and the creatures that are in it and surround it have this capacity for reflecting the divine omniscience. The throne room of God is a seeing chamber where omni-directional vision is given to those who enter.

The throne of God is a place where righteousness is loved and exudes like a mighty rushing spring unto life. From there proceeds the Messiah, who hates wickedness and whom God anoints with the oil of gladness above all His fellows. The throne of God is also the place where fragrant garments are made which exude fragrances of myrrh, aloes, and cassia. These garments come out of what is called "the ivory palaces," to make both the LORD and the wearer glad (Psa 45:6-8).

THE THRONE OF RULERSHIP

From the throne, God reigns over the nations of the world. Here God sits upon the throne of His holiness. Every now and then the princes of the people are gathered together; even the people of the God of Abraham. Who are the princes of the people of God who show up before the throne of holiness? They are the twenty-four princes who are mentioned as the foundations and gate-stones of heavenly Jerusalem. They are the ones who stand as God's shields over the earth, belonging unto God. In them, God is greatly exalted (Psa 47:8-9).

The LORD exercises His rule from the throne by sending the rod of His strength out of Zion (out of those who carry the constellation of His thrones). Through them, He rules in the midst of His enemies (Psa 110:2). From this throne, established and flowing through the constellations of those whom God inhabits, the day of the power of Elohim is manifested, displacing rebellion and making the people willing (Psa 110:3). From there, the beauties of holiness from the womb of the morning come forth and the dew of youth is cast upon the throne carriers. Here the irrevocable oath of YHVH is sworn and the everlasting priesthood order of Melchizedek is established: "The LORD has sworn and will not change His mind, "You are a priest forever According to the order of Melchizedek." (Psa 110:4 NAS)

From this throne, The Lord's right hand shall strike through kings in the day of His wrath. There is a brook flowing beneath this throne from which we shall drink in the way and our head shall be lifted up (Psa 110:2-7). From here, we shall have rule and shall no longer be under a tribute of any kind for, when we enter here, we are free citizens.

Heaviness will no longer cause our heart to stoop but access to the good Word of God will make the heart glad. From here flows the excellency of righteous ones, not capable of being seduced by the way of the wicked. The precious substance of diligence crowns the one who has access to this throne. In this throne lies the source and the way of righteousness, whose fruit is life and in whose pathway there is no death

(Pro 12:24). It is expressive of rulership - not just over vast arrays of idealistic terrains but also of rule over his own spirit (Pro 25:28).

THE FOUNDATIONS OF THE THRONE

There are four foundations of the throne of God: 1) Righteousness; 2) Justice; 3) Mercy; and 4) Truth. These four principles are essential to the throne. Upon them lay the canopy of the throne, as they constantly interweave before the face of the Most High, forming a habitation for God's throne (Psa 89:14).

In describing the atmosphere of The Throne room, the psalmist tells us that there are clouds and darkness round about it. He again repeats the ideas that righteousness and judgment are the habitation of His throne. In addition, while the throne is moving upon the waters, a fire goes before Him. This fire is what is called a consuming fire. It burns up His enemies round about.

Every demonic power or sinful being not washed in the blood of the Lord Jesus Christ, who does not contain the DNA signature of YHVH (the LORD God), gets consumed because she/he does not bear the record. From the center of the throne God's lightning flashes enlighten the world and the minds of those who bear the mark of the blood. People on earth may not recognize the emanations from the throne. However, the earth itself, having an intrinsic connection with the heaven, sees the movements coming from the throne and trembles.

The movements of the throne above terraform the earth. The hills melt like wax at the presence of the LORD - at the presence of the Lord of the whole earth. The heavens declare

His righteousness, and all the people see His glory (Psa 97:2-6). As such, for any throne to endure forever as a reflection of the supreme throne of God, it must also have as its foundation the four foundations (or pillars) of Righteousness, Justice, Mercy, Truth and His throne (Psa 89:14 and Prov 20:28).

OTHER THRONES

THE THRONE IN MAN

Whatever God is in macrocosm, man is in microcosm. The human being himself is a throne surrounded by a constellation of thrones - in the midst of which God the Three-in-one sits. If a human being has been washed by the blood, so that in the center of his being the lamb of God lays as though slain, the book of the Divine Prophetic is opened and which God uses to removes the dark serpentine spots from the human being. The redeemed individual's being structure corresponds to that which was written in the book of God for their lives from the foundation of the world.

Israel carries a type. Israel is in her constellation around the tabernacle and the whole earth is in a constellation around Israel. The constellations of various galaxies surround their sun or suns. So the heart of man, who is inhabited by God through the blood of Jesus Christ, is constellated by thrones over which he serves as vice-regent for God Almighty. He vibrates the rulership frequencies of the twenty-four dimensions of the heavenly city as he matures and manifests the intertwining spiral of his divine sonship.

THE THRONE OF INIQUITY AND THE RIGHTEOUSNESS OF KINGS

The Scriptures speak of a Throne of Iniquity (Psa 94:20) which is a seeking to rule without connection to God in the center. Those on this throne cannot have fellowship with God because it has as its modus operandi a framework of mischief and wickedness. This framework of wickedness and mischief is the distortion or mockery of the acts of God in creation.

The Word of God is the instrument that frames the world towards righteousness, peace and joy in the Holy Spirit. The Word is life and spirit. It frames the world for love, goodness and righteousness. The Throne of Iniquity uses words to frame mischief and evil, to bombard creation with negative vibrations in order to distort the divine image within it.

Whenever nations pass laws that contravene God's Word and let loose degrading laws, they are keying directly into the Throne of Iniquity. Out of every concentric intertwining constellation of thrones proceed words and thoughts. Words and thoughts from thronal interactions become laws or rules which serve as ground for rulership. When words and thoughts are not grounded in righteousness, they create a constellation of evil and confusion.

David knew this so very well from his experience with Saul and the kings of the nations where he lived as a fugitive, that he was led to ask:

> **"** This person must remember that every throne in his or her constellation must flow in "mercy and truth. They must answer the center of his/her essence, which is the image and likeness of God. **"**

"$_{20}$ Shall the throne of iniquity have fellowship with thee, which frameth mischief by a law?" (Psa 94:20)

Those who become the throne of the Most High (the dwelling place or the seat of God's rest) upon which constellations of lower (or service) thrones revolve, all directed to the glory of God the Father, must carry themselves as King. He must know that it is an abomination for kings to commit wickedness. Every constellation of thrones around him must be established by righteousness and must be committed to the divine essence in him, not to mere personality projections (Prov 16:12).

This person must also develop 'eyes' (allowing all the eyes within the body, soul and spirit to be cleansed and focused), for every throne must be a seeing device. Thus "as kings/rulers, they sit on their throne of judgment, they can scatter away all evil with their eyes" (Prov 20:8).

This person must remember that every throne in his or her constellation must flow in "mercy and truth. They must answer the center of his/her essence, which is the image and likeness of God. It is mercy and truth that preserve one as king/ruler/prophet/priest and uphold the throne upon which God the Almighty has placed him or her (Prov 20:28).

CONSTELLATIONS OF THRONES

The paradigm of constellations of thrones that I am espousing here is found in Israel's political structure in the Bible, notably in Psalm 122:1. This is a Song of degrees of David, which seem to be psalms of ascendency into the heavens. They are reflective of what is above and what Israel is to reflect upon the earth, especially in verse 5:

1 "I was glad when they said unto me, Let us go into the house of the LORD. 2 Our feet shall stand within thy gates, O Jerusalem. 3 Jerusalem is builded as a city

that is compact together $_4$ *Whither the tribes go up, the tribes of the LORD, unto the testimony of Israel, to give thanks unto the name of the LORD. $_5$ For there are set thrones of judgment, the thrones of the house of David. $_6$* Pray for the peace of Jerusalem: they shall prosper that love thee. $_7$ Peace be within thy walls, *and* prosperity within thy palaces. $_8$ For my brethren and companions' sakes, I will now say, Peace *be* within thee. $_9$ Because of the house of the LORD our God I will seek thy good." (Psa 122:1-9)

In the New Testament the Lord Jesus affirms this idea of constellations of thrones in the following words:

$_{28}$ And Jesus said unto them, Verily I say unto you, That ye which have followed me, in the regeneration when the Son of man shall sit in the throne of his glory, ye also shall sit upon twelve thrones, judging the twelve tribes of Israel $_{31}$ When the Son of man shall come in his glory, and all the holy angels with him, then shall he sit upon the throne of his glory. (Mat 25:31) (Mat 19:28).

What Jesus says here is a reference to the way the thrones of Israel were set up in both in the wilderness journey and in the Davidic and Solomonic dynasty. In the wilderness, all the occupiers of the thrones where called princes (Numbers 7), of which the chief was the High Priest Aaron or Moses, who may have been considered the king among them. This is also made clear in the way Solomon sets up the throne in his palace.

$_{17}$ Moreover, the king made a great throne of ivory and overlaid it with pure gold. $_{18}$ And *there were* six steps to the throne and a footstool in gold attached to the throne, and arms on each side of the seat, and two lions standing beside the arms. ₁₉ And twelve lions were standing there on the six steps on the one side and on the other; nothing like it was made for any *other* kingdom. (2 Ch 9:17-19 NAS)

Biblically, Israel is the earthly archetypal reflection of God's intent, but a similar pattern is also found in the way many ancient kings organized their thrones. Ancient kings who came into dominance would bring conquered kings that they favored (those they did not kill) to their palace. They would then place them on thrones below their own throne, as a revelation of their own superior kingship.

Take, for example, the treatment of Jehoiachim by Evil-Merodach king of Babylon. The passage clearly shows that the king of Babylon had constellations of thrones around him, each one having a special relationship with the king.

₂₇ Now it came about in the thirty-seventh year of the exile of Jehoiachin king of Judah, in the twelfth month, on the twenty-seventh *day* of the month, that Evil-Merodach king of Babylon, in the year that he became king, released Jehoiachin king of Judah from prison; ₂₈ and he spoke kindly to him and set his throne above the throne of the kings who *were* with him in Babylon. ₂₉ And Jehoiachin changed his prison clothes, and had his meals in the king's presence regularly all the days of his life; ₃₀ and for his allowance, a regular allowance was given him by the king, a portion for each day, all the days of his life. (2 Kings 25:27-1:1 NAS)

THE THRONE OF GLORY OF THE MESSIAH

The Lord Jesus tells us that, in the regeneration, the Son of man shall sit in the throne of His glory (Matt 19). Every throne carries its own glory. The greater glory belongs to the Father who gave it to the Son, as we read:

> "I glorified thee on the earth, having accomplished the work which thou hast given me to do. And now, Father, glorify thou me with thine own self with the glory which I had with thee before the world was." (John 17:4-5)

This throne of glory is not just the inheritance of the Messiah but of those whom God "raiseth up" out of the dust *and* "lifteth up" from the beggarly condition, from the dunghill. Those whom God has dealt with in this way He sets among princes. God makes them inherit the throne of glory and makes them the pillars of the earth, upon which He as the LORD sets worlds.

There are twelve glories of man in the lower heavens upon which man must practice kingship until he comes into the City and receives the other twelve; these complete him as the City of the Living God, combining the Patriarchal (lower heaven) and the Apostolic (higher heaven) (1 Sam 2:8). We will start to deal with these twelve glories of the lower heaven in the second part of this book.

JERUSALEM AS THE THRONE OF THE LORD AND THE THRONES OF THE NATIONS

The uniqueness of the Jerusalem lies on several facts. One

very important one being that the city itself is considered God's throne upon the face of the earth. As with most thrones of kings the people gather there for justice and for compassion - and so is Jerusalem to be. The Jerusalem of their time was a far cry from the reflection of the throne of heaven whose pattern it was to be. A throne, as the quote below indicates, would be a place from which the law is issued and principles are laid down for the ordering of righteousness and peace and, if necessary, war. However, the Jerusalem that Jeremiah describes is a far cry from this. Instead, out of it flowed everything contrary to the archetype whose reflection it was to be.

At that time they shall call Jerusalem the throne of the LORD; and all the nations shall be gathered unto it, to the name of the LORD, to Jerusalem: neither shall they walk any more after the imagination of their evil heart (Jer 3:17).

And He said unto me, Son of man, the place of my throne, and the place of the soles of my feet, where I will dwell in the midst of the children of Israel for ever, and my holy name, shall the house of Israel no more defile, *neither* they, nor their kings by their whoredom, nor by the carcasses of their kings in their high places. (Ezek 43:7)

As a result the Lord declare that He will cause other thrones to be set at her gates. These thrones will reflect that which this city herself had conceived by unrighteousness. These shall be the thrones of the opposition and of pain.

$_{15}$ "For, lo, I will call all the families of the kingdoms of the north, saith the LORD; and they shall come, and they shall set everyone on his throne at the entering of the gates of Jerusalem, and against all the walls thereof round about, and against all the cities of Judah." (Jer 1:15)

The Throne of the Haylel, the king of Tyre (one of the Shatan), the Throne of Babylon, and the Throne of Egypt are the three major thrones of the nations that we know. However, there are thrones in Assyria and Edom, and thrones of the sons of the east, of the south and of the North. All these thrones are often in rebellion against God and His purpose.

$_{13}$ For thou hast said in thine heart, I will ascend into heaven, I will exalt my throne above the stars of God: I will sit also upon the mount of the congregation, in the sides of the north: $_{14}$ I will ascend above the heights of the clouds; I will be like the most High. $_{15}$ Yet thou shalt be brought down to hell, to the sides of the pit. $_{16}$ They that see thee shall narrowly look upon thee, *and* consider thee, *saying, Is* this the man that made the earth to tremble, that did shake kingdoms; $_{17}$ That made the world as a wilderness, and destroyed the cities thereof; *that* opened not the house of his prisoners? $_{18}$ All the kings of the nations, *even* all of them, lie in glory, everyone in his own house. $_{19}$ But thou art cast out of thy grave like an abominable branch, *and as* the raiment of those that are slain, thrust through with a sword, that go down to the stones of the pit, as a carcass trodden under feet. (Isa. 14:13-19) $_{31}$ And it came to pass in the seven and thirtieth year of the captivity of Jehoiachin king of Judah, in the twelfth month, in the five and twentieth *day* of the month, *that* Evil Merodach king of Babylon in the *first* year of his reign lifted up the head of Jehoiachin king of Judah, and brought him forth out of prison, ₃₂ And spake kindly unto him, and set his throne above the throne of the kings that *were* with him in Babylon. (Jer 52:31-32)

₁ Come down, and sit in the dust, O virgin daughter of Babylon, sit on the ground: there is no throne, O daughter of the Chaldeans: for thou shalt no more be called tender and delicate. (Isa 47:1)

Daniel foresaw the casting down of the thrones of the nations and all their constellations. The only thrones that shall abide are the thrones that flow from and receive their authority of rulership from the Throne of the Ancient of Days.

₉ I beheld till the thrones were cast down, and the Ancient of days did sit, whose garment *was* white as snow, and the hair of his head like the pure wool: his throne *was like* the fiery flame, *and* his wheels *as* burning fire. ₁₀ A fiery stream issued and came forth from before him: thousand thousands ministered unto him, and ten thousand times ten thousand stood before him: the judgment was set, and the books were opened. (Dan 7:9-10)

THE CHERUBIC THRONE

The Cherubic throne is mentioned in Ezekiel. "Then I looked, and, behold, in the firmament that was above the head of the cherubim there appeared over them as it were a sapphire stone, as the appearance of the likeness of a throne." (Ezek 10:1) We see that the cherubic throne serves as the moving vehicle of the son of the man who is intimately connected with God. The cherubic throne shall be addressed in an upcoming book where we shall look into the mystery of the sons and what the cherub stands for.

THE THRONE OF GRACE

That there is a throne of Grace is clear from the following passage.

$_{16}$ Let us therefore come boldly unto the throne of grace, that we may obtain mercy, and find grace to help in time of need. (Heb 4:16)

One does not go boldly to the throne of judgment. In fact, when the King sits on His throne of judgment there is fear and trepidation. The throne of grace speaks of the clear confidence of sonship which has been bequeathed to us by the life, death, resurrection and advocacy of the our Lord Jesus Christ

EXPERIENCING THE THRONES

If the Throne of God is established in the heavens and the Kingdom of God rules over all of them, then it behooves us to consider that our earthly perspective is too small a telescope to look into the mysteries of the heavens. The Kingdom of God, though manifesting on the earth, is not confined to the little portion of the universe called earth, especially if we consider earth in its current state. It has something to do with the current earth only as the transitional note to a new earth, and mainly because it is the training ground for the human being who bears the record of the DNA of God in the created universe.

The earth, as it is currently, is not the Kingdom of God and is never going to be the Kingdom of God if it stays as it is now. It must pass through the fire so that it will be able to handle the imposition of the schematics of heaven upon it. In order to reconnect it to the heavens this old earth must give way to a new one. The Kingdom of God that the psalmist is talking about here (Psalm 103) is the whole universe: "His kingdom rules over all."

If His kingdom rules over all, we can infer that He sets His throne in the heavens in all the dimensions of time and space and in every dimension of the heavens. He sets thrones for those whom He has appointed kings and priests. In every dimension of heaven He sets a specific throne for Himself. In my vision of heaven I noticed that the throne of God in heaven is unique, so much so that there is no other throne that can compare with it.

There are thrones in other dimensions of heaven and they do not look the same (wherever I have been taken in the spirit). If you have had experience of thrones in the sprit, even the colors and designs of the thrones do not look the same. Sometimes one looks like jasper, another like beryl and another is glowing amber like the sun.

> **"** If His kingdom rules over all, we can infer that He sets His throne in the heavens in all the dimensions of time and space and in every dimension of the heavens. He sets thrones for those whom He has appointed kings and priests. **"**

The variety of thrones in various dimensions of heaven seem to tell us that most ancient kings patterned their thrones after various thrones in the heavenlies and some even after the thrones in the underworld.

Most thrones of kings on earth were designed and patterned after thrones seen in visions by seers, shamanic priests or prophets. Have you had an experience where you have actually been to different dimensions and seen thrones in the spirit? If you have seen thrones, you may have noticed that the thrones do not look the same every time you go into the realm of the spirit and see them.

First, they do not look the same because you who see and experience them are not the same every time you go into the vision. They also do not look the same because God is always showing the variety of the beauty of the heavens through the thrones. Furthermore, they do not look the same every time you enter a vision because you may be seeing thrones in different thrones.

When I have conversations with some people who have visions of heavens, I often hear them describing varieties of colors and configurations in the thrones they have seen. You may say, "Oh, it is not real - it is just in their imagination." I do not deny that. However, imagination when put in motion by the Spirit, is the concretization of the archetypes of the spiritual realm in the psyche of man. The truth is that you experience the throne based on your relationship with God and based on where you have been in the spiritual realm.

God created us in such a way that we can experience different dimensions of the universe

> **"** God created us in such a way that we can experience different dimensions of the universe in God by ourselves in the inner-space of our being where God lives. The experience may appear unique. **"**

in God by ourselves in the inner-space of our being where God lives. The experience may appear unique. So unique that it may seem we are the only ones who have ever been in that dimension (and that nobody else has ever been there).

Since we are operating as human beings in this world, the way we think, our faith-imagination and the framework or window through which we experience the world and God (including our faith-imagination) open us to experiencing God and the various dimensions of the universe in greater or lesser authenticity.

ANGELS

The Bible speaks of angels or beings that are in direct relation to the protocol of heaven. We commonly call them all 'angels'. The term 'angels', as one of the writers of the Christian pseudepigrapha (an early Christian writer), Dionysius of Areopagus, states, is a general term used for beings that are diverse, distinctly designed, in their being and their functions.

Every dimension and every heaven has angelic structures. Angels are assigned to particular aspects of the universe - even on earth. An angel is usually assigned to do more than one thing at a time.

Angels do not cross dimensions of duty unless by the direct command of a higher authority. They may go from one dimension to another but they do not change their duty. When you begin to deal with angels, if you try to change their duty you get yourself into trouble. One of the reasons people don't get results when they encounter angels is that they try to get angels to do what they were not sent or created to do.

I am not talking about the demonic, the fallen angels. The demonic function and cater to the whims and lusts of man, in opposition to God. The demonic are mimickers. They do not obey the structures of God. They try to change the way the structure works (however, they must follow the principles set down by God in order to obtain any results). That is what witchcraft is. Therefore, you have to make a distinction between trying to be a magician and actually trying to relate to God and allowing angels to serve you for the purpose of the kingdom and your salvation.

When we deal with angels we must remember that there are heavenlies (plural) - at least we know from Paul that there are three. However, my understanding of this is not that there are three heavens or seven heavens but that every dimension of the heavens are reflective of the triadic interconnections (or inter-circularity) and resonance frequencies. These 'threes' and 'sevens' then move to 12 and then to 24 - but the one where the ark dwells is always the one standing in the center or on top, depending on how you look at it.

Even from the Book of Genesis 1:14-20 there are various heavens or dimensions of heavens. My understanding of the heavens from Scripture and from visions is that there are structures of nested heavens. These nested heavens are often manifested in interlocking nested ecologies of three structures. As I am Trinitarian in the prism by which I look at the universe, I see each dimension in the imagery of the 3 in 1 Godhead (as man is in body, soul and spirit when he's restored and reconciled). His trinitarian nature is an interlocking of triadic spiralling circularity. I speak, therefore, of ecologies of nested heavens within heavens as a way of communicating my view of the complexity of the heavens.

By the word, I refer to beings that may be called beasts and other strange looking creatures who do the will of God, ministering to God and ministering to humanity - until humanity comes to the fullness of God and the fullness of Jesus Christ is fulfilled. Angels are meant to operate with us in certain ways as tutors (Gal 4:1-2) until we come to the fullness of what God created us to operate in.

When the Bible uses the word 'angel', it is usually referring to all the structures of the angelic. The angels that most people know of are the ones who are named, but there are more than that.

Angels have strength, they have power and they have superhuman strength. Most angels are one-dimensional. A few angels are multi-dimensional. In addition, here is something you have to understand - angels do not have free will. The angels that we know now do not have free will. An angel with a free will is a demon.

So if you are able to manipulate an angel to do what you want it to do when it comes to give you a message, you are not dealing with an angel from God - because angels from God are answerable to the Master. Now there are angels that are sent to you to do specific things with you. They are given permission to do what you ask them to do but you really cannot make them do anything contrary to the will of God.

This is the reason why the church does not teach on this topic. It is because people then start being active in areas that they should not be active in. They may be able to handle it personally but they mess up other people.

In Psalm 103 it says, "Bless the Lord ye angels that excel in strength, that do His commandment hearkening unto His voice." Keep that in mind. Then he says, "Bless the Lord all ye His hosts." Why would the Bible use the word "angel" and then use the word "hosts?" Because the word "hosts" is the Hebrew word Sabaoth. The word 'Sabaoth' refers to a particular kind of being. They are not angels. (There may be an 'angelic Sabaoth' however, which is a 'multitude of angels').

There are angelic beings that have within themselves what you discovered in the demon-possessed man in Matthew - that they are legions by nature. Remember, Jesus said, "What is your name?" He said, "*I* am legion, for we are many." He did not say, "*we* are legions" in plural but "*I* am legion". They have the capacity in themselves. There are myriads and myriads of beings put together who can actually release all kinds of realities. Usually, these are creatures used for warfare by God.

Remember, whatever you find in the dark world, there is always the original counterpart in the world of light. Remember, out of every category of beings that God created, one-third of them fell (Revelation 12:4). That is what the Bible tells us - when Satan fell, he took one-third of the stars with him. Here's the good news. There are more angels than there are demons. Two-thirds of the angels still abide with God.

Back to Psalm 103; "Ye ministers of His, that do His pleasure." What is a minister? A minister is someone who serves directly - a servant. Many of the beings you see that come and do things for you are servants; they are ministers that God sends. Preachers are also ministers. Some preachers are ministers, some preachers are hosts. Some preachers are angels, depending on where they occupy in the scheme of what God is doing. We speak in the New Testament of apostles, prophets...it is the same thing. They are categories. It is just the name that changes.

So, understand that my use of the word *angels* does not mainly refer to what we generally refer to as angels in the western tradition - beings that look like men but differ only in the strange protrusion of wings and feathers growing from their shoulder blades.

(For greater discussion on angels I refer you to the series on angels and their function at www.aactev8.com or you can purchase the book on angelic structures).

THE ECOLOGY OF THE NESTED HEAVENS

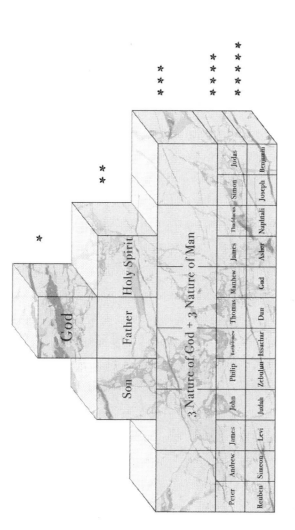

*	1	- The Echad Dimension: The Person of God (not a heaven) Deut 6:4
**	3	- The Trinitias Dimension: God in 3 Persons (not a heaven)
***	6	- The Divinity / Human Intersection Dimension: The Embodiment of God in Man (a created heaven of 6 dimensions)
****	12	- The Upper Kingdom Intersection Dimension: The Sons Of God (a created heaven of 12 dimensions)
*****	12	- The Lower Kingdom Intersection Dimension: The Sons of Israel (a created heaven of 12 dimensions)

AN OVERVIEW

Now let us consider the diagram. The highest dimension is the Echud '1'Dimension. This is the very person of God. Next is the Trinitas '3' Dimension which is God in 3 persons. The "Trinitas Dimension" and the "Echud Dimension" equal four - Yod-Heh-Vav-Heh.

You can not get into these dimensions. They are not 'heavens' as they are not created. They are dimensions of the person of God Himself. You can only see these dimensions from afar. You may experience this dimension a little bit, but you can't get into it.

The heavens are a created reality to help man know and experience the loving, infinite God. God is not heaven or contained by the heavens (1 Kings 8:27, 2 Chron 2:6 & 6:18).

These first four dimensions of the Echud '1', Trinitas '3', all have to do with the mysterious nature of God. These dimensions can not be entered by anybody anyhow. There is nothing you can actually do. You can say all you want to say about knowing God, but you only know Him so far. For all eternity you will be trying to learn this. It is like approaching a horizon. You keep getting close to the horizon, and what happens? It keeps moving. The more you grow, the greater God gets. You are never really going to know the depths of God.

When Paul says that we see as in a glass dimly, that's true here. Even in the heavens, you see more clearly, but you are still seeing from a glass because you are still learning to become like your Father. 1 Corinthians 15:27 says, "For he hath put all things under his feet" God will put all things under His feet. What will happen at the end when all things have been put under the feet of Jesus Christ? Then Christ will give up and subject Himself to God the Father, and then God will be all in all.

We won't understand the separation of the Trinity when we get there because everything will be one. The distinction of the Trinity, even in its intrinsic nature and the way we see it now is not how it's going to be (once the redemption of the earth has been accomplished, we have come to the point of knowing who we are and we've matured as sons). The stepping out of the Son in eternity by the incarnation of Christ - so that we could actually recognize the Son as a separate being - is something that happened because of the creation of man, so we might know what our inner nature ought to be like.

Next is The Divinity / Human Intersection '6' Dimension. This heaven is the first of the created heavens. It's 6 dimensions are the embodiment of God (3 dimensions) in man (3 dimensions). This '6' Dimension is where God wants man to be. However, human beings will never get there while they're alive because this means that they have become the 'heavenly man'. It is what Paul meant when he wrote "when that which is perfect appears, then we shall be like Him." (1 Cor 13:10)

I know we say a lot of the time, "We are already like Him". True, we have His nature in us but we have not been able to break through to this level because we are not yet glorified. It's because we still have flesh and blood.

" I know we say a lot of the time, "We are already like Him". True, we have His nature in us but we have not been able to break through to this level because we are not yet glorified. It's because we still have flesh and blood. "

Now, there is a demarcation here between the '6' and the '12' Dimensions. The Divinity / Human Intersection '6' Dimension really is Adam in the Garden of Eden. When man fell, God did not begin man again at 6. He began with man at the Lower 12 - so this is where you can actually go right now. The two '12' Dimensions are the highest you can go, but 90% of the people who know God will never even get there. To be clear, we are not saying that no living human being can access the '6', rather when a living human operates in manifest and matured Sonship all that belongs to the Father is open to them.

The Upper Kingdom Intersection '12' Dimension is where God is revealed in ever expanding space - this becomes the cubic city of the New Jerusalem, a living organism. This is not creation as we would currently understand it, but it is created all the same. This heaven and all it's dimensions are intended for you to explore. However, we must concentrate on the Lower '12' Dimension first in order to access the upper dimensions. We have not yet come to the Upper 12 Dimension. (Just know it is there for future reference, as 12 above plus 12 below is 24 - and there are 24 in the Kingdom of heaven and in the Kingdom of God).

The Lower Kingdom Intersection '12' Dimension is where a Christian will first find themselves and so it is here we will focus in this book. This is where God is revealed in static material creation - creation as we traditionally know it. There are 12 dimensions in this heaven that you have access to. Even though you are (subconsciously) everywhere because you are in God, this is the first level you can consciously interact with. As you intentionally engage with these 12 dimensions you will mature and be able to consciously access higher heavenly dimensions.

THE DIMENSIONS ARE INFINITELY EXPANSIVE

That is a brief introduction to the Ecology of Nested Heavens as shown in the diagram. If you look at the diagram, it is a pyramid, reaching down and ever-expanding. However, as God at the top of the pyramid is unfathomable in size, and so actually the largest dimension, it is also a pyramid going up. A pyramid going up and a pyramid coming down - which is the expansiveness of God and the dimensions He has created.

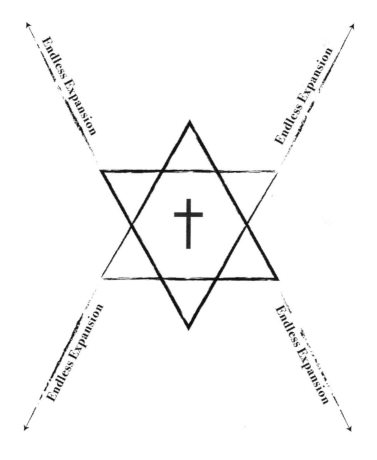

The pyramidic expansion going down and the pyramidic expansion going up is what the Star of David actually is. The fact that the Star of David diagram stops on top doesn't mean that it actually stops in reality. It is just an imaginary line and is not closed - as it is truly infinite expansion - up and down.

THE LOWER KINGDOM INTERSECTION '12' DIMENSION

$_{12}$ "It had a great and high wall, with twelve gates, and at the gates twelve angels; and names *were* written on them, which are *those* of the twelve tribes of the sons of Israel.

$_{13}$ *There were* three gates on the east and three gates on the north and three gates on the south and three gates on the west.

$_{14}$ And the wall of the city had twelve foundation stones, and on them were the twelve names of the twelve apostles of the Lamb.

$_{15}$ And the one who spoke with me had a gold measuring rod to measure the city, and its gates and its wall.

$_{16}$ And the city is laid out as a square, and its length is as great as the width; and he measured the city with the rod, fifteen hundred miles; its length and width and height are equal.

$_{17}$ And he measured its wall, seventy-two yards, *according to* human measurements, which are *also* angelic *measurements.*

$_{18}$ And the material of the wall was jasper; and the

city was pure gold, like clear glass.

$_{19}$ The foundation stones of the city wall were adorned with every kind of precious stone. The first foundation stone was jasper; the second, sapphire; the third, chalcedony; the fourth, emerald;

$_{20}$ the fifth, sardonyx; the sixth, sardius; the seventh, chrysolite; the eighth, beryl; the ninth, topaz; the tenth, chrysoprase; the eleventh, jacinth; the twelfth, amethyst.

$_{21}$ And the twelve gates were twelve pearls; each one of the gates was a single pearl. And the street of the city was pure gold, like transparent glass." (Rev 21: 12-21)

The City of God in the Book of Revelation has 12 foundations. Let us begin there and work backward. God says to Abraham, your children shall be "as the stars of heaven" Gen 15:5. However, Abraham only has nine children. Understand that 9 represents the keepers of the gate at every dimension. We find that among some cultures of the world reaching the tenth level of any spiritual venture is considered to have attained perfection in that venture. In that case 9 is considered the 'transition to' and hence carries the possibility of beauteous and harmonious transformation or a moment toward judgment. In Christianity, according to the New Testament, there are nine fruits of the Spirit which serve as the gateways for entrance into the number ten which, as I have come to understand it, is the entrance into sonship, heirship and the fullness of God as spoken of in Ephesians 3:19.

The nine fruits of the Holy spirit are the things God uses to teach and train us as we prepare to enter completely into the fullness of the Father's being. These 9 fruits are then also keys that let us through the gates that allows us to cross into greater experience of the realms of God our Father. In some ancient numerical system 9 represents nine gods with the highest of them being the tenth. This ancient system maybe behind the 9 high court judges who represent the gateway in the United States Supreme court to legal harmonization. They close the gate to certain ideas or open the gate to certain ideas. They allow certain things or they close certain things. It is also a principle in some ancient thought systems. However, the nine are not the heavenly dimensions. The nine are the gateways to every heavenly dimension.

Note that God tells Abraham he is going to have children like the "stars". Yet Abraham has 9 children, so he doesn't really catch the stars - that is he does not have 12 or 13 children, but 9. They serve as a transition and preparation for the emergence and entrance of the star system of God into the world with Jacob in the future. Isaac stays and has two children - Esau and Jacob. Esau carries the negative possibility. Esau has a lot of children, but he spends his time building a kingdom without building character. He receives a kingdom before Jacob receives a kingdom. In fact, he has 30 kings (Gen 36:31-) before Jacob has even come out of slavery. Jacob is still serving Laban while Esau has 30 kings reigning on Mt. Edom. Esau represents the heavens that you create on your own by your carnality that must be destroyed.

They must be destroyed because they're shells. They are empty shells. I am making this practical to you now. They are shells and they must be destroyed. Esau is also the purification of the negative junk DNA that Abraham carried from Babylon. God is separating the light from the darkness, separating until he gets to the heavens. In your life you want the 12 dimension to emerge. You cannot enter this dimension until you have dealt with yourself, until you have dealt with that shell, that junk you have been struggling with. Even when Jacob is the chosen one, he still has to deal with himself because there is something still left in him that God wants to work on.

When Jacob comes to Padanaram and gets really close to where Abraham began in order to re-enact the journey of Abraham back to Canaan. When Jacob marries, he marries two women. He marries one because he likes her. The other one he marries because God forces him to marry her. God gives her to him, with the help of Laban. It is the one he did not want that becomes the mother of the Messiah.

Jacob now has 13 children - not 12. These 13 children represent the patterns of the heavens, of every lower heaven, which is 13 zodiac signs and 13 star systems for every heaven. So in the city, which is the city of Lower heaven (heaven in the earthly manifestation), God has shown us that the heaven that we can access has 12 patterns. That is the first thing that was shown. The 12 patterns have to deal with 12 dimensions of relating to God. It's a 13 pattern which results and it is the gateway for manifesting in the 12 pattern. Why? Because the 13th is a woman, Dinah. It is the 13th that you must protect because a stranger wants to rape her (Gen 34) in order to cause her to bring forth something that is not in your destiny.

In that heaven, there are 12 basic principles. In fact, in every dimension of this heaven, these 12 dimensions are where you still have to deal with negative aspects of your character/DNA. The nature of 12 dimensions are revealed when Jacob blesses his son in Genesis 49. As we understand and process these 12 dimensions with God, it will deal with our fallen nature, allowing us to rule as kings and sons. As we understand the nature of the twelve sons we will understand the nature of these dimensions of heaven and thus the elements we ourselves will need to address in our lives.

The reason God reveals Israel the way He does is because He wants to teach you about heaven. He's not teaching you about earth. It is a pattern where He shows you exactly what He's doing in heaven. Israel is the revelation of what God is doing in the supernatural realm.

Based on my experience and the way I've studied Scripture, the heavens that God reveals to us, whether they are infinite or not, are always divisible by three and four. (This is based on the nature of God and the name of God). This 12 dimensional heaven is set out in four sets of three nested heavens.

Below is the same camp diagram set out in linear fashion. You can clearly see the four sets of three. Moving through these dimensions is not a hierarchy or process of enlightenment, like an eastern religion, or a system of works and achievements. It is a working with the Holy Spirit to remove

> **"** You can clearly see the four sets of three. Moving through these dimensions is not a hierarchy or process of enlightenment, like an eastern religion, or a system of works and achievements. **"**

the fallen DNA nature from your life so as to reveal your true nature. Many steps can be worked on simultaneously but some are more foundational than others. To not address them will cause them to appear later in your life. The order follows the birth/camp order of the sons and was set by the wisdom of God.

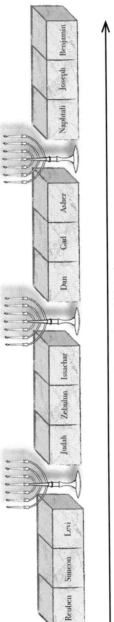

Progression of Maturity

THE LOWER KINGDOM INTERSECTION '12' DIMENSION

So, the way you can study this heavenly dimension is to study the sons of Israel. (After you can consciously engage the Upper 12 Dimension, based on the apostles). We will deal more with this in an upcoming book.

When you start to experience and mature in the first dimension of this realm, which is represented by Reuben, you can move to the next dimension. You move to Simeon. Then to Levi.

We need 3's, and we need 4's. So, in the first three dimensions we have Reuben, Simeon and Levi. They are like a trinity. Three separate entities, yet the trinity is still one.

MOVING FROM ONE HEAVEN TO ANOTHER

Remember, the structures of heaven are revealed in how God sets patterns in Scripture. We have talked about the different levels or dimensions. I do not like the word *levels*. The term *dimensions* is better - because levels sounds like somebody's stacking layers up on top of another. Dimensions are intertwined, interwoven, interconnected.

Dimensions are non-intersecting streams - either in consciousness or in space. You cannot really get into them unless you are jarred from one stream to another. You can not usually move into a dimension at your leisure. Accidents cause you to move to the next dimension.

> " Remember, the structures of heaven are revealed in how God sets patterns in Scripture. We have talked about the different levels or dimensions. I do not like the word levels. The term dimensions is better - because levels sounds like somebody's stacking layers up on top of another. Dimensions are intertwined, interwoven, interconnected. "

Pain causes you to move to the next dimension. Suffering causes you to move.

As you pursue the realities of God and there is a crisis in your life, the crisis moves you to other dimensions. Nobody moves from one dimension to another without a crisis. It's just like a rocket that does not move from this orbit to another orbit without propulsion and without fire. First the natural, then the spiritual. Most people do not purposely jump from one dimension to another. You do not slide to the next dimension - you get knocked into it.

We have a tendency to sleep in every dimension we find ourselves. You want to go to sleep there because you are just like Peter, "Let us build a tent up here." God responds, "No, not on this mountain. This is not yours. You cannot build a tent here."

Dimensions are non-intersecting. They are parallel. There are gates that connect dimensions. But not everybody can find the gates. Most people who move from dimension to dimension do so through suffering. Some people find the gates themselves. That is what I am trying to help you do - to find the gates to get in a new dimension. It is not always through suffering. It is possible to purposely move from dimension to dimension, through the gates.

However, you are going to suffer anyway. I hate to tell you this. It is not always the devil that makes you suffer. It is God's way of making sure you know how to wake up. If pain does not happen to you, you will never wake up. Your first broken heart taught you what love was. You may not like it, but it's true.

The gate is a gate that is in your body, in your feelings, in all your emotions. The gates must be opened and the gates are opened by suffering. "Take up your cross and follow Me," says

Jesus. Does that mean you should be sadomasochistic? No. This is why people miss the point. You don't need to run into a monastery and go hide yourself and starve yourself to death in order to be able to have this. Life will happen to you.

God has so orchestrated life that the cycle of your life brings you pain and suffering. At every moment that you come into the context of suffering, you have to make a choice according to how you're going to respond. When you respond to that little bit of suffering that happens to you, in the way you're supposed to respond to it, then a gate opens for you to move to the next place. It is daily life. If you're engaged in daily life, if you're engaged in relating to people, you're going to be tested - in the daily work of your life, in your workplace.

This is why real Christianity does not really demand that you go and become a monk. It demands that you live life, that you live life with thoughtfulness and intentionality and that you pay attention to everything. That you do not go through the world as a zombie. "Awake thou that sleepest, and arise from the dead, and Christ shall give thee light" (Eph 5:14).

THE 12 AND THE 13

Now, we know God is one and God is three in one. We also know that God created humanity on the sixth day. So numerically, man is 6. However, there is also the 7 and the 5 in the center.

I will tell you why I'm not dealing with the higher dimensions. It is difficult for human beings to actually deal with the '6', '3' and '1' Dimension levels - because we really haven't mastered ourselves. You would think that you should be able to master the smallest first. Or that it's easier to deal with '1'. However, you're not ready to deal with Echud '1' Dimension because, in God's scheme, 1 is everything.

The reason the two '12' Dimensions, Upper and Lower, are divided into triad nested heavens is so you can navigate them easier. The Echud '1' Dimension will overwhelm you. God is One. That means God is in everything. God is everywhere. Your consciousness is in a plane where you currently can not handle a higher level. It does not mean you're not in it. You are already in it. However, you cannot handle it with the consciousness you have right now. Therefore, the two '12' Dimensions are given to you as an easy way to navigate. Symbols are given all around you to support the 12.

It sounds contradictory if you think about it. You should be able to handle one thing first, but the immensity of God doesn't allow you to do that. God uses the two '12' Dimensions, Upper and Lower, to train you. Remember, the first heaven that man can actually grasp in this fallen state is the Lower '12' dimension. You go through the Lower 12 in order to go up to the Upper 12. So There are 24 dimensions in this heaven. As you process through, you understand how the12 is related to the 24, and how the 24 is related to the rest of the higher heavens - God in his fullness.

When you begin to master the various dimensions, you will find yourself beginning to move into your oneness with God. However, if you strive to become one with God, you end up going backwards.

God has made it so that, when you deal with issues, the dimension looks like it is infinite, but it's not. In dealing with it, you're able to understand inter-relationship. By understanding inter-relationship, you are able to get into a place where you actually understand your oneness with God.

To talk about your oneness with God without dealing with your issues in these dimensions and all the other dimensions is to actually become like Lucifer. It's to think you can be God in the sense that God is God. God teaches you the distinctions and the varieties so that when you become one, and your consciousness gets tied into the divine, you don't get yourself into hubris. You do not speak from hubris. You don't think you have really arrived or that you know everything.

Twelve is where we start. God uses 12 for the Old Testament patriots, sons of Israel. Jesus chooses 12 disciples. However, there is actually 13. There is always 1 that is sitting there. When you get to heaven as described in the Book of Revelation and you look at the heavenly beings, you find 24 elders.

However, there is one that looks like the Son of Man sitting upon the throne. Therefore, the two 13's that are both in the Old Testament and in the New Testament become one. 2 equals 1 because the scripture says in Genesis chapter 2 "therefore the man will leave his mother and father and cleave to his wife and they two shall be one."

God placed the '12' in everything in our whole system. He has placed 3, 4, and 12 in our system. There are twelve months in a year. (Thirteen months actually. However, one is not a complete month. It needs four years to become whole). The day is 24 hours. (There is also a fraction of it that is completed every leap year.)

So the whole system is around you. You find it in the Zodiac system. The Zodiac system is based on God's system. However, you are not meant to use it as astrology to try to divine. That will get you into all kinds of trouble. That is not the reason for the zodiac. You need to think of this rationally and, in a sense, scientifically. God put the signs above you for a purpose.

So 24 is 12 and 12. There are 12 below. There are 12 above. As in heaven, so it is on earth. There are 12 patriarchs 'below' and 12 apostles 'above'. 12 hours of the day, 12 hours of the night. 12 and 12 making 24.

The structure of the heavens have different dimensions. Man was created in the image of God. He was closer to God, so there was no distinction between the first three levels (1, 3, 6) and the 12. However, in the fallen world, the 12 dimensions are the heavens you can actually experience quicker.

GOING DEEPER: 12 AND 24

We are talking about the heavenly dimensions. Let's take some time to read Revelation 21 again. It is the foundation of what we are learning and your gateway into the realms God has made for you.

"And I saw a new heaven and a new earth, for the first heaven and the first earth were passed away. And there was no more sea. And I, John, saw the holy city, New Jerusalem, coming out of heaven, prepared as a bride adorned for her husband. And I heard a great voice out of heaven saying, 'Behold the tabernacle of God is with men and He will dwell with them and they shall be His people and God shall be with them and be their God. And God shall wipe away all tears from their eyes and there shall be no more death, neither sorrow, nor crying. Neither shall there be any more pain for the former things are passed away.' And He that sat upon the throne said, 'Behold I make all things new.' And He said unto me, 'Write, for these things, these words are true and faithful.' And He said unto me 'It is done. I am the Alpha and Omega, the beginning and the end and I will give unto him that is athirst of the fountain of the water of life freely. He that overcometh shall inherit all things and I will be his God and he shall be my son. But the fearful and the unbelieving and abominable and murderers and whoremongers, sorcerers, idolators, and liars, shall have their part in the lake which burneth with fire and brimstone which is the second death."

And there came unto me one of the seven angels who had the seven vials full of the seven last plagues and talked with me saying, 'Come hither, and I will show you the bride, the Lamb's wife.' And he carried me away in the Spirit to a great and high mountain, and showed me that great city, the holy Jerusalem, descending out of heaven from God, having the glory of God, and Her light was like unto a stone most precious, even like a jasper stone, clear as crystal. And had a wall great and high and had twelve gates, and at the gates, twelve angels, and the names written therein which are the names of the twelve tribes of the children of Israel: on the east three gates, on the north three gates, on the south three gates, and on the west three gates. And the wall of the city had twelve foundation, and in them the names of the twelve apostles of the Lamb.

And he that talked with me had a golden reed to measure the city and the gates thereof, and the wall thereof. The city lieth four square and the length is large as the breadth. And he measured the city with the reed: twelve thousand furlongs. The length, and the breadth, and the height of it are equal. And he measured the wall thereof: one hundred and forty-four cubits, according to the measure of a man, that is, of angel. And the building of the wall of it was of jasper and the city was pure gold, like unto clear glass.

And the foundations of the wall of the city were garnished with all manner of precious stones: the first foundation was jasper, the second sapphire, the third chalcedony, the fourth emerald, the fifth sardonyx, the sixth sardius, the seventh chrysolite, the eighth beryl, the ninth topaz, the tenth chrysoprase, the eleventh jacinth, and the twelfth an amethyst. And the twelve gates were twelve pearls: every several gate was of one pearl. And the street of the city was pure gold, as it was transparent glass."

And I saw no temple therein, for the Lord God Almighty and the Lamb are the temple of it. And the city had no need of the sun, neither of the moon to shine in it, for the glory of God did lighten it. And the Lamb is the light thereof. And the nations of them which are saved shall walk in the light of it and the kings of the earth do bring their glory and honor into it. And the gates of it shall not be shut at all by day for there shall be no night there and they shall bring in the glory and the honor of the nations into it. And they shall in no way enter into it that which defileth, neither whatsoever worketh abomination or maketh a lie, but they which are written in the Lamb's Book of Life." (Rev 21)

When I begin to talk about the structure of heaven, I know what I am talking about - when I talk about the 2 (major levels) we have immediacy of access to, the 12 and the 24, I take it directly from this chapter.

The person who has salvation, who knows God, is able to access 24 dimensions in the heavenly realm. 24 dimensions. That is precisely why you were given 24 hours in a day. Even though you have 12 months in a year, you actually have 24 months because you have the New Moon and the Full Moon. Or you might actually have the moonless part of the month, and the moon part of the month, which divides it into two. It is the same principle.

The 24 principle reveals the structures of the heavens that are knowable to man. These structures of the heavens that are knowable to man first of all must begin within man.

There is a heaven in man. Not every human being can actually be called a 'man', Adam, because most human beings are not rational. If human beings are dead in sin, they are dead. Therefore, 90% of the human beings living on earth are dead. They are dead in their sins and trespasses. Forget about the fact that maybe 1 or 2 billion Christians live on the face of the earth - that is just the name. Over 80% or 90% of them are still asleep or dead. Moreover, 5% of those who are awake are only partially awake. They see wrongly.

They cannot really see a dimension where they are actually awake. Their sight is still from the sleeping dimension. They still have sleepy eyes. They are dream walking. The other ones who are awake are scared of the ones who are still sleeping!

Let's come back to the text because I do not want people to think that I am just making this up. These things are in Scripture but people do not want to ask, "What does it mean?" They just want to think that God does things just because God does things. Everything that God does has a purpose. Every act of God is complete and beautiful. Every revelation of God is complete and beautiful.

We are dealing with the tribe of Israel as a basic foundation of understanding and also as heavenly dimensions. Remember, each of these tribes has a gate. They open a gate in terms of your physical feeling dimension, your emotional dimension, your intellectual dimension and the supreme intuitive dimension, which can sometimes be confused with the voice of the Holy Spirit. There is a need to work on making sure that man's highest intuition is not confused with the supreme voice of the Holy Spirit. Remember however that the effects of various places in the heavens impacts the traveler in different ways. With all the experiences of dimensions of heaven, God is working and revealing something about you because there is really no heaven / heavenly experience without you.

God does not need heaven. He does not need earth. He does not need any of these. God could have been God for all eternity without you and me. Everything else that is experienced is created because of you. That is God's way of having you experience a dimension in God.

It is an ecology of nested heavens - heavens within heavens within heavens within heavens - that are relating to one another and allowing you to experience the different dimensions of God. You have been born again. You have been born into God. Now you need to start experiencing the different dimensions of God as you come into the fullness of who you are. As Christ gets formed in you, you get filled with the fullness of God.

> **"** You have been born into God. Now you need to start experiencing the different dimensions of God as you come into the fullness of who you are. As Christ gets formed in you, you get filled with the fullness of God. **"**

God wants you to test the different dimensions of what He has in store for you. However, it won't taste good if you are still carrying the taste of your former dead life. This is not to bring you salvation. That has been done. This is not to redeem you. That has been done. This is to make you enjoy what has been given to you. You must understand, I don't believe you can do anything to save yourself but I believe you can be saved and not enjoy what has been given to you. There will be people in heaven who are going to be crying because they never really had the opportunity to experience, in their former life, the kinds of areas God wanted them to experience. There are going to be tears in heaven. That is why the Bible says God will have to wipe the tears away (Revelation 21). It is because there are a lot of people who are satisfied with just being born again.

THERE IS MORE

Christians do not realize it is just the beginning. It is like a child that is born and stays a one-day old baby. He can never really walk on his own. He cannot really eat and enjoy an apple. You know what I'm saying. You must enjoy the different dimensions of life in order to be a full human being.

The same thing is true with the Kingdom of God. God wants you to enjoy the different dimensions of His being. That is why the Bible says, "Oh, *taste* and *see* that the Lord is good." The things God wants you to experience about God - you have no clue how available God is to you.

When we are talking about heavenly dimensions we're not just talking about something that's going to come in the sweet by and by. There is going to be a lot of things in the sweet by and by, however, right here and now, there are also things you must experience - things that you need to experience to get you excited.

So there are 24 dimensions we can readily access. That is man. Because 24 (2 + 4) equals 6, the number of man. Remember in the center is always somebody. One person. So 24 + 1 = 25, and 25 = 7, perfection, completion, rest. Everything God gave Israel to unfold on the material level reveals the spiritual dynamics that are going on in the life of God. So they were put in symbols to allow you to experience certain things. We could look at this even in the call of Abraham.

Abraham and Sarah are one because husband and wife are one. Abraham has two children, in the beginning. Then he gets seven other children. Therefore, he has nine. One of them, Ishmael, is a judgment principle who is always fighting with everybody else. Isaac has two children, Jacob and Esau, but something happens to Esau.

Remember, earlier we saw Esau goes and does his thing and has about 30 kings before Jacob even has anything. Jacob has 13 children: 12 sons and 1 daughter. He becomes the paradigm for the heavenlies. However, until Jacob, who is the 3rd level, is himself transmuted to the Man that sees God, Israel, he is unable to bring forth the spiritual principle inherent in him. Jacob is the 3rd level (third ancestor) and also the man level (6 dimensions). So then, it is 1 and 3. Then from Jacob (6) there is a shift immediately into the two '12 Dimensions'. The 6th is bypassed because man is fallen. Then there's 144. You might think that 144 only deals with the people that are chosen from Israel to go to heaven. However, when the city's wall and aspects are measured it becomes 144. What is 144? 12 squared. So it is still the number 12. In other words, even though we are dealing with 24, heaven is an expansive dimension by the number of 12, always divisible by

3 and 4. You want to experience the '12'. If you were a Jew and you had a true experience of the mystical nature of what God is revealing in the tribes, you also had access to the Messianic process. If you didn't get what was carried with the 12 tribes and with the tribe of Levi, the 13th, chances are you did not really get the Messianic principle. We can draw from this some other things.

Remember in the Book of Leviticus and the Book of Numbers, where the ephod is put upon the priest. It represents the dimensional movement of God in the lower realm. It takes both the upper realm and the lower realm to make one heaven; above and below unify to make one heaven. The lower realm of the heavens is accessible to the human souls who have actually disciplined themselves. This is where Christians, and many people who are not Christians, get offended. The truth is they do have access to that realm because Israel was meant to be priest to the nations. On the day that the Lord God divided the inheritance of the nations of the world, He numbered them according to the numbers of the children of Israel. That is in the Bible.

> "When the most High divided to the nations their inheritance, when he separated the sons of Adam, he set the bounds of the people according to the number of the children of Israel." Deut 32:8

In other words, every nation on the earth has access, by virtue of birthright, to a particular dimension of the lower heaven. But the nations have not worked on a lot of this, so they bring with them the unclean water and their anger. They bring whatever it is that is part of their terrible DNA or the monster DNA of their ancestors into that heavenly realm.

This is the realm where you encounter all that warfare - demons and dragons and serpents. There are things unleashed by men and women whose birthright is that heavenly dimension but who have not yet been purified. Therefore, they come up there and they leave residues of their monster DNA.

Human beings, in their natural capacity, have access to particular dimensions of heaven because the Bible says that man cannot receive anything unless it is given to them from heaven! In addition, when you confuse yourself by thinking that unbelievers do not have access to heaven, you have to ask, "Which heaven?" The truth is that Native Americans have access to a particular kind of heaven that allows them to prosper all of a sudden. When they have access to that heaven, they can prosper beyond any other group of people. The only natural people group who have access to all the dimensions and to the 12 lower heavens are the Jews, because they carry the mark upon their body.

> **"** Every person, every tribe, every family on earth has access to a particular heaven. It is difficult for them to cross over from one dimension to another because God puts - are you ready for this - the flaming cherub in the gateway to make sure they don't cross from one point to the other. **"**

Every person, every tribe, every family on earth has access to a particular heaven. It is difficult for them to cross over from one dimension to another because God puts - are you ready for this - the flaming cherub in the gateway to make sure they don't cross from one point to the other. The flaming cherub is in their body - the very thing that allows them to access that dimension also hinders them because they have not worked through their issues/DNA.

What God did by taking Israel into Egypt, putting Israel in bondage for 450 years, was the process of suffering that purified Israel. Even after the 450 years Israel was still not ready. So God takes Israel through the wilderness and allows them, in those 40 years, to traverse the different heavenly dimensions. Read it very well because Israel was not really in the earth dimension when it was traveling through the desert. If it was, you would be hearing of wars. You would read of wars from the beginning until the end. However, you don't hear of many wars because of what God was doing. That's why the Bible says, "Those who saw My miracles in the wilderness." (Numbers 14:22) Which miracles in the wilderness? Those who were tested, are those who saw.

The Bible makes a correlation between those of us who have seen the heavenly dimension and who've tasted the glory of the world to come, but we don't believe and we will fall away - there is no salvation for us since there's nothing else God can show us because God has shown us Himself.

That's why God destroyed a generation in the wilderness - because they had seen God. They had participated in the heavenly realm and yet still refused to believe. That is also why you cannot know what happens to the people who have not seen Jesus, who didn't know Jesus was coming, because the access to the heavenly dimension gives them a particular consciousness of who the Messiah is. They always want to create the Messiah for themselves because they have a shadow of it in them.

Now 24 also represents your hours of the day. We who are modern forget these things but ancient cultures, including early Christianity, prayed according to the hours because every hour of the day is a gateway to a particular dimension and creates an alignment to a particular dimension of heaven. God puts this concept in everything, so that you know.

Once again, the problem we have is when we are wakened in one dimension, we like it so much that we stay right there. As we mentioned earlier, it is like Jesus on the Mount of Transfiguration with His disciples. Jesus was with the three and boom! - Jesus appears for who He actually is. They see Him, they are awakened. They are forced into awakening but they do not understand what that means. Even though they are awakened to the transfiguration of Jesus they are not awakened to other things about the life of Jesus. So they want to stay there. Actually, they want to stay there and fall asleep in the experience. It is a hard thing. However, in every awakened consciousness, if it is a body consciousness, or if it is an emotional consciousness, or if it's just a mere feeling consciousness, you need to pay attention.

Even in the motion/movement of consciousness of your body you do not walk just because you walk. You walk and pay attention. Kings are trained to walk intentionally, and so are queens. They are trained to put on clothes intentionally. They do not do anything just to do it. They eat intentionally. They chew intentionally. They put their mind into what it is that they are doing. Most of us do activities just because we do. To move through the gates we need to be aware and intentional about our lives.

SUMMARY

We have been studying the structures of heaven and how to navigate them. We have been studying what we call the ecologies of nested heavens. This is meant to give you a kind of technology for navigating the heavenly region and for really understanding how it actually functions based on the Bible and not based just on what you think. It is based on an objective provision that is hidden within Scripture itself. God's patterns are in Scripture.

God does not do things just because. He does things in order to have us understand. There is a statement Paul makes which is a statement that is common to most mystical schools of thought. The statement is, "First the natural, then the spiritual." It is a very strong principle. We think spiritual, then the natural. If you don't understand nature, and you don't try to deal with nature, you will not really grasp the spiritual. It doesn't mean you need to study a lot of nature. It means that the things that God has revealed in Scripture, which look like natural patterns, are actually heavenly patterns.

The Scriptures were not written by any private interpretation. They were written as the Spirit of God moved upon man. In other words, they have a divine principle within them. They carry within them the structures and patterns of God. We carry this Book around and all we do is quote it to hit each other and make each other look bad, rather than actually knowing what is in it. We use it as a principle for defending our 'un-thought' through opinions.

We have been speaking of the heaven as paradigmatic of self-construction, self-creation, self-constituting, self alteration, self-transformation. We are talking about affirming the self in its divine nature. Not the self that you have created, that you are pretending to be. We are talking about your divine self, which is cluttered by all of your associations, identifications and things you have made up. We're talking about your Christ nature transcending all the illusionary selves that you have created.

That is what heaven is. Heaven is seeing God as God is and standing before God naked and not ashamed. That is what the Garden of Eden is. Until then, you are using activity to cover yourself. You are using religion to protect yourself, using the pretense of spirituality to cover yourself and using a lot of other things to hide your nakedness from your real self and God. You're using laughter to cover yourself. You are using false seriousness to cover yourself. It's all the same thing. That is what we have been doing throughout our lives.

We have been doing what our father and mother did in the Garden. Every day that is what we do. We try to cover ourselves. God knows that. That is why God wants to be your clothing. Any other covering, apart from the real self, which is Christ, still leaves you naked. It is like covering yourself with leaves.

You and I need to deal with some things in our lives. You have to ask yourself some very serious questions. First, you need to ask yourself, "What depends on me and what does not depend on me?" You need to be honest about what actually depends on you and what does not depend on you.

Absolutely nothing depends on you. Absolutely everything depends on you. Oops! When you understand that, you actually begin to be productive. Is that contradictory? Nothing depends on you because the world will go on. If you fall and die today, we will go on tomorrow as if you never existed. Yeah, your wife may cry for you for about two or three years. She is not crying for you because you really matter. It is because she misses you. Her feelings miss you. You are gone. So you need to get real about what it is that really matters. What can you really do? Breathe? Is it you that is breathing, or is the machine called your body breathing? You will still go on existing when that body stops breathing. At least that is what Christianity teaches.

We have to come to a point where we actually understand that all things depend on us and nothing depends on us. Do you think that if you stop talking to the person that offended you that the person's life is going to stop?

MOVING IN THE HEAVENLIES

I want to deal with some very important principles when it comes to traveling and moving in the heavenlies. When you deal with the structures of heaven, it has to do primarily with a subjective change of position. Not an objective change of position. There is a reason you cannot experience what another person experiences in heaven. You cannot relate to the spiritual experience of another individual unless that person tells you what they have experienced. Then it becomes a subjective principle in you.

God will show you things in heaven. I will go up there and I will not see those same things. The only things that we all see in common are the things the Scriptures describe. We see the lampstand. We see the throne. We see the gold. We see all the scriptural references. Why do we see them? Because the Scriptures have spoken them and embedded them in our consciousness. That is why when we get up there, they manifest to us. However, regarding all the other aspects we see, very few of us see the same thing.

Tell me if I am wrong. I'm willing to listen. Some people go to heaven and do all kinds of activity. You go to heaven, you see the candlestick, you see the throne, you see the Sea of Glass. Where did you hear about that? In Scripture. However, when God takes you into different rooms that are not mentioned in Scripture, you come back and tell us and many of us go up there but we don't see those rooms. Why? Because God creates the experiences you need in order to experience Him the way you need to experience Him. But the 12 heavens, the 12 dimensions are there. You cannot experience the dimension you need to in order to experience God the same way others do. You experience them the way that God wants you to experience them.

Consider, what is Reuben's problem? Lust. We will see this clearly in a few chapters. But what is lust? It is nothing but passion and desire. It is not sex. It is lust. You can lust after money. You can lust after power. You can lust after many things. Every time you say *lust*, the church think sex because the church has come up with the idea that every sin is sexual. It is not.

Lust is the agitation of the instinct powered by self-talk or powered by situations. Lust is empowered by what people believe is important. What people say you should have in order to be important. That is what lust is. Then you begin to lust for a commission. You begin to lust for people. You lust for appreciation. You go after it for recognition. As we will see, that is Reuben.

We need to understand how in every heaven, there is a hell embedded in it. If you don't like that reality, you are not going to be able to deal with yourself. Whichever dimension of heaven you go into, if you have this glorious experience but it never raises the issue of you dealing with yourself then you have a problem. Every dimension of heaven you get into calls attention to something in your humanity that you must come down and deal with in order to effectively manifest the truth of that dimension.

Just because you are shown revelation does not mean you have the capacity to manifest. You have to ask yourself, "What keeps me from manifesting?" Every time a dimension of heaven is shown to you, you need to ask yourself the question, "What hell do I need to walk through in order to actually have it manifest?" What hell did God have to walk through in order to create the earth? It is right there in Genesis 1:1-3. Chaos, death, non-productivity.

We are going to look in-depth into the heaven and hell of each of the 12 dimensions. The first 6 are contained on this book. Reading this carefully and applying it to your life, as opposed to getting purely an intellectual understanding, will help you identify and overcome troublesome areas of your life. These are the areas preventing you from moving through the dimensions and revealing your true self as a Son of God. I promise you, it will be challenging but very, very rewarding.

SECTION 2:

THE FIRST 2 TRIADS OF THE LOWER KINGDOM INTERSECTION '12' DIMENSION - THE 12 SONS OF JACOB

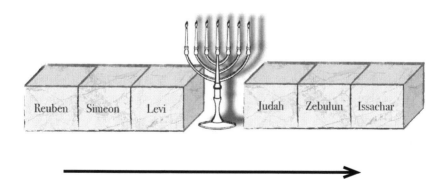

THE PRIESTHOOD TRIAD
– REUBEN, SIMEON AND LEVI

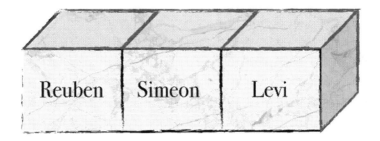

The 12 dimensions of the Lower 12 are split into groupings of 3, or 'triads'. So we have 4 triads, giving us the 3, 4 and 12. Each dimension follows the sons of Jacob as he blesses them in Genesis 49 and the Israelite camp layout in Numbers 2 . Let us look at the first triad of the Lower 12 Dimension and their natures as they are revealed in the blessing of Jacob. As we understand the natures connected to each of these dimensions we will be able to process them in our lives. This will free us from the lower or fallen nature of each son / dimension and release us into our true nature.

> **"** As we understand the natures connected to each of these dimensions we will be able to process them in or lives. This will free us from the lower or fallen nature of each son/dimension and release us into our true nature. **"**

THE PRIESTHOOD TRIAD		
Son:	Son:	Son:
Reuben	Simeon	Levi
Meaning:	Meaning:	Meaning:
Excited/Excellent	Heard	Joined
Dimension:	Dimension:	Dimension:
Sonship	Judgement/Severity	Priesthood
Persona:	Persona:	Persona:
Judgement	Wisdom	Understanding

⟶

REUBEN - THE DIMENSION OF SONSHIP AND JUDGMENT

"Reuben, thou art my firstborn, my might, and the beginning of my strength, the excellency of dignity, and the excellency of power: Unstable as water, thou shalt not excel; because thou wentest up to thy father's bed; then defiledst thou it: he went up to my couch." (Gen 49:3-4)

God structures the heavens according to what He reveals to us in Scripture. Let us begin with Reuben, as the first principle. I am using Reuben as an example. I'm not saying Reuben is a heaven. I'm saying Reuben is a representation of the system of a particular dimension in heaven. Everything God reveals to you on earth is designed so that you can understand things in the other realms. Because you have not been there, God is the only one who can give you a pattern for understanding it.

In the 'Reuben dimension' you are navigating a heaven of sonship. Now if you are the firstborn, you have the birthright. So let's just assume you are the firstborn. That is what our sonship is. We are all operating in sonship. In this heaven you have a right to provision. You have a relationship where God just gives you access to inheritance because of your birth position. You are experiencing things because God gives you access because of your birth position. You also have access to things that belong to your Father alone. So what is the danger? Reuben sleeps with his father's wife.

What is the greatest struggle every new Christian has? Come on, be honest – it is sexuality (don't act as if you do not know this). It is lust. If you were already married when you became a Christian it's different, but you still deal with it. Something gets activated in you. When we first became Christians, most of our confession was "Lord, take this sin away from me. Take this sin from me." Why? Because the problem is in this Reuben dimension. In this ecology of nested heavens, in this heaven of sonship, you have so many rights given to you. However, you are not ready physically.

Now let's say you are Reuben and you have access to everything as the firstborn. In this dimension is a lake and this water must remain stable and must be stirred rightly in a certain way at the right time. We should be careful not to agitate the waters wrongly as Reuben did. If you agitate the water, it swallows you. The thing about Reuben, the thing about this heaven, is that its waters are so strong. When you look at the set heaven, the waters are like crystal. There is a crystal sea. They really don't move.

So what gets activated? Lust gets activated. When his father Jacob blesses him, he says "Your issue, Reuben, is that you are as unstable as water." He says "You are the excellency of my strength; you are the beginning of my dignity. You are everything I want, but you are unstable".

So how do you navigate this section of the heaven? How do you navigate this sonship capacity? You navigate it by trying to steady the water. But here's the thing – you cannot steady the water because the water is you. This is the reason why Jews emphasize the control of the circumcision point for men and virginity for a woman. A woman has the capacity to keep herself and make sure that she's not operating in such a way that the waters are so stirred up that she cannot inherit. The result of operating carelessly in this dimension is losing your firstborn right.

The more spiritual you are, the more you need to deal with this. The first place God releases you as a believer is into this Reuben dimension of heaven. You pray for somebody to get healed. You do this miracle here, you do this miracle there. As a result, you get yourself involved with people that activate your instability. In this dimension, the issue is not the devil. The issue is you.

So how do you then deal with this area? This is where you need the angels whose elemental principles are water. Now this is my perspective. I

> **"** You navigate it by trying to steady the water. But here's the thing - you cannot steady the water because the water is you. **"**

believe the reason for Reuben's failure is that his father did not teach him how to access that aspect of his 'angelic being'. That is - you are not dealing with an external angel, you're dealing with yourself. Because there is an angel that is you - a reflection of who you are.

Remember when James is talking, he says, "For if anyone is a hearer of the word and not a doer, he is like a man observing his natural face in a mirror; for he observes himself, goes away, and immediately forgets what kind of man he was" (James 1:23-24 NKJV). The reason we fail in this area is because we are so afraid of looking at ourselves in the face. It is a shame. And the reason is because of shame. Now I'm going to help you if you are a firstborn child. We will talk about heaven, but we're going to talk about you as a firstborn child.

There's so much responsibility put upon you that you know a lot of failure in your life. I mean presumed failure. Sometimes your parents put it on you. Sometimes you put it on yourself. That expectation that you put on yourself actually creates a problem for you.

I can tell you that your problem is mostly sexual. It is true. The people who are not firstborn don't understand. The reason is that it is a principle of validation - because you have not navigated your heaven very well and your parents did not help you to navigate it the way you needed. When you come to the spiritual realm, your sonship is so powerful that you will need to face a couple of problems. You have a problem with instability and you have a problem with not respecting boundaries.

REDEMPTION IS THE PURPOSE

> **"** People in the movie industry have greater insight than people in the church. **"**

In every dimension of heaven you walk into, you are going to have to learn this reality - especially in the beginning. This Reuben dimension is where you learn it. The father judged Reuben. He did not kick him out. He judged him unto redemption.

I'm going to give you an example of how Reuben was redeemed. In mysticism, people teach that you need an opposite, a negative principle to release the positive principle. In this particular case, nothing can help unstable water except water. Only somebody with power over water can control a person who is unstable.

> **"** Everybody operates in a particular kind of heaven, whether they do so intuitively or by actually seeing it. You are there whether you like it or not. **"**

That is why Moses was appointed to redeem and restore Reuben. In Deuteronomy 33, Moses, when blessing Reuben, reverses the curse of Jacob by saying, "let Reuben live. And let his people be many." Moses was the one with power over water.

Angels, like everything in the universe, are formed in different elemental structures. Some are water. People talk about water spirits. There are water spirits that are fallen angels. There are angels who are literally made of water. There are angels that are flames of fire. There are angels that are spirit, which are winged. When you get into a place like the Reuben dimension, you begin to see beings.

People in the movie industry have greater insight than people in the church. They show you beings that are made of water and that are made of crystal. Don't say that's not possible. Don't you think that, since the world is 80% water, that there are water beings - that you are a being of water, and that there are other beings who are also beings of water?

The 12 dimensions are not separate from each other. They are just dimensions. It is not as if you're going to go to a heaven, as you might go to a house. Then you jump from one house to another house down the street. They are interconnected one to another. When you navigate one dimension, then God reveals another one to you.

There are some heavens that are such a test that they are

quicksand for you. So you need to struggle. You need to deal with your nature so you don't get swallowed up. Do you know that people in the church - who don't travel to heaven inside - are still operating in the heavens? Everybody operates in a particular kind of heaven, whether they do so intuitively or by actually seeing it. You are there whether you like it or not.

Remember the Bible says that you and I are seated in heavenly places. Do you know that you are sitting in heavenly places? There are people who can actually see where they are in heaven. There are people who cannot see. Just because you can't see, doesn't mean you are not there. You are there.

You find people struggling with the same dimensional issues repeatedly. It is because they're stuck in that dimension of heaven. God wants you, once you get acquainted with a particular dimension and you overcome what it is, to grow. Then you literally shift dimensions. However, you don't lose the experience you have of this heaven because it is a cumulative experience.

The key is to accumulate as much as you can because it's fun when you get more experience. For some of you, every time you gather together to go into the heavenlies, you're going to the judgment throne of God. You don't need to do that all the time. You need to experience different dimensions. Now you still need to have your training as a judge so to judge things, but you don't need to do it every time you gather together.

ANGELS AND HEAVENLY PROTOCOL

Let me show you some things that you can work on in this particular Reuben dimension in the structures of heaven.

Watch for the positive. Look at the words to Reuben:

"You are my firstborn. My might. The beginning of my strength. The excellency of dignity. And the excellency of power. You are unstable as water. Thou shall not excel because thou wentest up to thy father's bed. You defiled it. He went up to my couch."

> **"** What God is trying to do is to teach you protocol. **"**

Reuben needs to learn how to respect boundaries. We must learn how to respect boundaries. Angels in this realm are teachers. They tell you, "Oh no, you can't do that". Now if you have ever traveled in the dimensions and experienced the heavens, you noticed the first time that you wanted to touch something they tell you, "Just wait. Wait, wait son." This is because there is something about you that needs to change. It is not because it doesn't belong to you.

What God is trying to do is to teach you protocol. There is a protocol. If you don't practice that protocol here, it's going to be difficult for you when you get up to other dimensions and higher heavens. You can't get up to heaven, see Gabriel and say, "Hey Gabriel, come over here." You will get yourself in trouble.

Do you notice that people who met an angel in the Bible called the angel 'Lord'. This dimension is where you learn the language of protocol and where you learn to deal with these protocols. Even though you are a son, you're still under tutelage (Gal 4:1-2). Even though you are a son or daughter and you're going to reign forever, you are still being taught. But if you think you're somebody and you get there and you start acting, then you enter into hubris. Remember, the more potential you have for greatness, the greater the potential for evil.

Some of you have traveled to heaven without dealing with yourself. This is your reason for non-manifestation. You need to deal with these angels of this area. You need to understand the excellency of your own strength. The reason boundaries are set is that this is where you train yourself for rulership because a man who rules his spirit is greater than a man who rules a city (Prov 16:32). A person who rules himself is greater than a person who rules a nation. God is training you so you understand how to move delicately in dimensions.

BECOMING FREE IN MATURITY

We are dealing with this thing that we call the physical body. Part of the problem with the Reuben issues is that it is tied to your body. That's the thing. It is tied to your physical body, your physical desires, your physical feelings.

The truth is you have an illusion that you are making decisions and choosing actions - but you are not because you are not free yet. Actually, we are used to thinking of sexuality as the big thing, but in every part of our lives, we are controlled by what is already happening around us. This is the heaven where God puts you in touch with who you are. It is a heaven where you experience. It is a heaven where you get to not like some aspects of yourself very much. It is a heaven where you wake up. This heaven is a womb, and you can sleep in it as long as you want. So many people stay asleep.

However, understand that the issue is this - if you're not careful, your experience of the heaven of this dimension will be mainly about what gives you pleasure. Most Christians live in what they enjoy and they think it is the will of God. They think it's God's will because it feels good. Pentecostals are really, really sold on that.

The immaturity among us is so amazing. We've got no capacity for submission. We've got no capacity to actually follow a real mentor. We think we are free but we are actually reacting to things. So when we fall, we fall heavy. Because we do not really deal with ourselves we spend most of the time judging everybody else - not looking at ourselves.

To us everything to us is about morality however this is not accurate. Everything is about choice. In this place, God shows you that you are a slave. If you're a person who wants to be asleep, God will let you enjoy yourself and never really experience the other dimensions of heaven because you have stayed a baby. You need candy. You need milk. Unfortunately, this is what we do.

When Reuben was mature, he had developed such bad character in himself that he couldn't even deliver his brother Joseph from the hands of his other brothers. He was waiting for them to leave so he could come and deliver the boy (Gen 37:22). He could not tell the truth to himself and, having failed so many times, he became ashamed of himself.

This is the dimension where you begin to deal with that mess in terms of the physical, actual behaviors that you are doing. God saves you, pulls you up to that dimension and begins to deal with you. The problem with many of us is that when God begins to deal with us, we step back. We don't let him deal with our junk because He reveals it to us and we have to work on it. He reveals it to you incrementally because you cannot deal with big things. You cannot deal with planets yet. You can only deal with little things at a time. In addition, when you begin trying to work on yourself by working on the big things, you always fail.

So you begin with the small things because you're going to

get discouraged if you think you can just transmute yourself from being selfish and self-centered. This is a good thing as you can stay selfish and self-centered if that's what you want! In fact, the universe will bend to help you stay that way because the universe does not want you to wake up either.

Everything in the world, including God, conspires to keep you asleep. God will make it as difficult as He can for you to wake up. God is not going to make it easy for you to wake up. If He really wanted to make it easy for you, He would have made Jesus descend from heaven with clouds of angels so that all of us could just say, "Yeah!"

God did not even reveal who Jesus was. He revealed this to a few kings and shepherds in the bush somewhere in Africa and Asia. The kings came down and saw Him and, when they wanted to tell the whole world, they were told to be quiet and go back home. They went back home. We didn't hear from them again - ever.

Do you get how God behaves and how difficult He makes things for you? God puts you through a training that you must do. You need to take responsibility for your choices. You have to choose to be something other than what you are. But in order to do that, you need to wake up.

BEING TRUTHFUL WITH OURSELVES

In experiencing the Reuben dimension, you're experiencing the watery heaven that comes with a lot of the things that have to do with water. What you want to do is to navigate this principle until you come to the four rivers of God - until you come to the source of the actual water.

I'm going to show you what I am talking about. Go back to

Genesis 49 and see these four rivers. Jacob calls Reuben My might (1), the beginning of my strength (2), the excellency of dignity (3) and the excellency of power (4). Don't count 'firstborn' - firstborn a position.

The key then is to harness, within that context of experience, the four rivers of God. To find a place of intimacy with God where you are naked before Him, you are naked before yourself, where you have nothing to hide.

David says, "I said to myself, all men are liars." (Psa 116:11) And it's true. All men are liars. You are a liar. I am a liar. We lie to ourselves. You don't tell yourself the truth. I don't tell myself the truth. I do not like it. No, we are liars. We do not know how to tell the truth. We could not know the truth if it hit us over the head.

Remember, Jesus did not say I tell the truth. He said, "I *am* the Truth." Why do we lie to ourselves? We lie to ourselves in so many ways. We lie to ourselves about our feelings. We lie to ourselves about what we actually know. We lie about what we know about God. What makes us lie is the fact that we are reactionary in the way we deal with the universe.

We are not operating from a place of sovereignty and freedom. Therefore, God causes us to learn how to tell ourselves the truth. You do not have to tell me the truth. However, you need to tell yourself the truth. We spend all our lives trying to tell people what we think is the truth about them. We are being trained to do just that for ourselves.

We react to things. If one operates by reacting to things, then one cannot be fully in the truth at all times. It means that one is living in half truth. That is, half of what one tells oneself is not true. It does not mean that you are an outright liar. But half of what we tell ourselves is true, and half of what we tell others is a reaction based on what we learned in school or tradition or hearsay (which will need to come under the scrutiny of the fiery flame of the cherubim) and our authenticity is lost. That is what I mean by lies. They are "untruths".

It is obvious that one can never think all of his/her reactions through. The information is true, but true at what level? Is it true because the teller has experienced the information in its reality, or is it true because they know the information by revitalize download? Some of you are saying, "If he's lying to us, why should we listen to him?" That is not what I mean. I hope you understand the distinction.

I'm telling you truth about God. I know it, because God has revealed it to me. Do you realize there are some things I'm telling you that I know, but I have not experienced? I hope that you know that there are some things I know because I have seen them, but I've not experienced them within myself.

You can have a vision and not have an experience. I have seen a lot of things in heaven, but I have not really imbibed them into myself. That God has blessed me to see visions does not mean that I know what I'm talking about. I am reporting to you what I know is there, right? However, a lot of the things I have looked at in the dimensions of the heavens I have never entered into. God just blessed me and said, "Let Me show you things. Now you go teach."

Therefore, I must tell myself the truth. Remember, when you are teaching this topic, you're teaching because God graced you with a revelation to help people and not because you know some intrinsic realities within yourself and are greater than them.

Some of these things I have experienced. That is why

I am scared of testimonies. You really cannot have a lot of testimonies without falling into embellishment. Now I do not think you just go out telling lies. I do not think you are a liar in the sense in which you are thinking. I am saying we are liars in the sense of not telling ourselves truth. Are you a truth teller? If I did something wrong now, you would tell me exactly what I've done wrong. If you did something wrong, you would not tell it to yourself - at least not with the same honesty in which you tell me.

So here in the heaven of Reuben God makes you look at yourself. Do you know why this is a watery place? It is because water is self-reflective. You can look at it a little and realize. "Oops... is that what I look like? I hope Johnny is not watching." That is what Reuben is about.

Then you understand what limitations God has placed upon you. Until you know your limitations, you cannot operate in your infinitude. I'm going to put it another way. This is where you come to the end of yourself. Until you know you are nothing, you cannot be something. This is where you come to nothingness. You come to nothingness when you say nothing exists - not even me. I don't have an identity. Then all those false centers that you have created begin to disappear and you end up going up and into the realm of the kingdom. This is the process of divine denudification - a type of openness and vulnerability to God.

DEALING WITH WHAT IS INSIDE OF YOU

You see, I don't have a problem with a lot of issues that other people have a problem with. Not because I am perfect but because of something I've learned. When it comes to you or me, as a person, there are things that need to be dealt with. If I don't deal with the things that are in me as a single individual I could cause a ripple effect in my community that will hurt so many people in the spirit realm. In the same way, the spiritual atmosphere of this city has been changed by my presence. I could have done other things to it. This fact of changing the atmosphere is not a matter of pride. It is just fact.

There has been a change since I stepped into this city three years ago. I've been working and operating in the supernatural realm to get people's minds to begin to focus on what it is that this city is supposed to be about. I no longer operate the way I used to, which was impatiently. When people come here and do their activities, I just laugh and I just keep doing what I'm doing. However, I could not do this many years ago because I was still in the heaven of Reuben.

Where you get in trouble is when you put yourself in a position of teaching when you're not ready to teach. Your instability attracts other people who are unstable. You cannot handle it and they mess up your water. Instead of seeing your own reflection, every time you see a reflection, you see their reflection - the person that messed you up. That's why every time you close your eyes, you are thinking of them because their reflection is in your water. However, if you use the Word of God, focus on the Word of God and you begin to speak the word in that dimension, then the Word of God which you have learnt and mastered become an angelic being. You tune yourself.

For example, it is in this place that God sends you people you don't like and tells you to love them. It is in this heaven that you encounter things you do not like and people you do not really like. You don't like them because what you 'like' is your god.

You are worshipping your capacity to like things. God conspires against you. He makes it difficult for you. And then, you want to go back to sleep immediately. "I don't like this - goodnight." That is what we do. In this place, God will send you things you don't like. God is not in the business of pampering you because God is growing a god in his image. Since God is growing you into a god, then God is going to put things before you. That is how God is.

Remember, God doesn't know anybody that God does not like. God does not operate by feelings. In this heaven you are going to have to deal with your feelings and people and situations that you don't like. You're going to not want to be with those people or in those situations. At certain points you can choose not to be with the people you like and stay with the people you don't like just so you can develop your capacity to tolerate things. That is what God does to you.

How many of you have been in a place where it seems like everybody that comes around you is someone that you don't like? You ask, "God, what did I ever do? Why are you sending me all these jerks?" It is because you need the jerk in you to be dealt with!

God is saying to you, "It's not that I like evil. It's not that I like people who don't do things right. It's just that I need to teach you how to be like me." If you do not like 'red', God is going to immediately take red and put it in front of you. Why? Because, if you like red, you do not need to make a choice. You have not developed your sovereignty. If you walk away from the red, your feelings are not going to get hurt. Therefore, you're not really doing life out of freedom - you are doing it because you are a slave to your feelings.

God is going to bring someone around you that you do

not like. Since you do not like 'green', God is going to put green in front of you. Now this is the catch. If you feel sorry for green, then you are still operating from your feelings. You don't like green, but you feel sorry for green. You put yourself in the center of green because you are feeling sorry. "If I leave green, what's green going to do now?" You actually think you are making a choice but you're a slave to your feelings. So what is the answer? The answer is, "Okay, I have green. I do not like green. I want to kill green. I want to put green in the grave. I want to kick green's behind. So I choose to spend five minutes with green and not do all of those things I want to do to green."

MOVING BEYOND YOUR FEELINGS

Do you see what I just did? Many of you give things to people because you feel sorry for them. You are not really a giver. You are just a slave to your feelings. You did not make a choice, but you think you did. Feeling sorry has kept many

> **"** Remember, God sends His rain upon the just and the unjust. **"**

people in positions that they should have been out of a long time ago. You did not make a choice as a sovereign individual.

Remember, God sends His rain upon the just and the unjust. This is the God who will let the child of a wicked man live and let the child of a righteous man die. These are the things people in church and religious people do not want to deal with. God does that every day. Is it not true? Haven't you seen this God in heaven...the One who is unmoved?

He loves the righteous person with all His heart but is unmoved by everything the righteous person does or cries over. Instead, what does He do? He gives something good to the person that is not even a believer. That's the problem that the writer of Psalm 73 and Solomon in Ecc. 8:14 and every righteous person that has ever lived has needed to deal with. "God - why do the righteous suffer and the wicked prosper?" It is because God is not moved by feelings. God acts sovereignly in every situation. Can you do that? Well, you cannot if you do not deal with this Reuben dimension.

> **"** You are feeling sorry for yourself / within yourself. **"**

This is where you train yourself to be a sovereign person acting from will, not from compulsion. This is where compassion is developed. Let's talk about compassion. We are told compassion is about feelings. Whose feelings? If it is about your feelings is it actually about the other person at all? See, it's about you. Compassion is being able to feel what the other person is feeling.

Most of what we feel is not compassion. You are just feeling sorry for yourself and do not know what the other person is feeling. You are feeling sorry for their condition. You are in their suffering. You need liberation.

Can you actually enter into the feelings of the other person? It takes discipline to choose to be in somebody else's suffering. That is why you can only handle it for a few minutes because it is about you. It's not about them. You cannot handle their pain for more than one day. What do you do when you see suffering children on television? It is not compassion that makes you give. You are feeling sorry for yourself / within yourself. Moreover, you are not making a sovereign choice. You give out of guilt. You do everything out of your own feelings. Whom are you doing it for?

I am just going to speculate for a second? Bilhah is a slave woman that became the wife of Jacob. Jacob probably did not treat her as a wife. So she goes to Reuben, who is the oldest son, and she was probably about Reuben's age. "Your father doesn't touch me. You know, when he does, he just treats me like a slave. Doesn't he realize I'm his wife now?" Reuben says, "I'm sorry, sweetie." He feels sorry for her.

This heaven is great because you can have all the pleasures you want. Nevertheless, it always comes at a price – because most of the pleasure you have at this level comes from your feelings, from your enslavement to your feelings. It is a heaven of your pleasure. It is a heaven of your feelings.

Many of the heavens you see are heavens of your own experience so that you can feel good. God responds to you. You want to get to the point where you say to God, "Look, Dad, I understand I got these feelings, but I want to see things that are different from what I'm feeling and what I've been told. I need to desire."

Believe me, I understand what these feelings say: "Show me gold dust." These feelings say, "Let the angels sprinkle dust on me and let's dance around." That is what these feelings say.

I do this. I am telling you, my feelings want this heaven because I want to enjoy these kind of things. "But Father – I want to move beyond what I'm feeling. I want to experience something that I have never experienced that has nothing to do with my feelings, even if it is painful. Take me to a new threshold. Take me to the crucible."

This is because to cross from here to Simeon is going to tear on your body. That is because there is a separation that happens from your flesh.

In dealing with these things in Reuben's heaven a good

protocol to deal with these things is vibrating the name of God "Yod, Heh, Vav, Heh". You build your house with the name of the Lord. The house that you build with the four-letter name of God is also the source of the four rivers that strengthen your water. It gets your water balanced. Then you read the Word of the Lord. You pick up the Word and you eat it. You eat the scroll of the Word. You swallow it.

It begins to balance your water. It turns your bitter water into sweet water. It gets you to begin to direct the water so that it flows in its course in your life. Then the next protocol is to ask for those angels that are present there, who deal with the moving of waters, with the dividing of waters and the bringing back of waters. They are there.

It is not a simple thing to free yourself from your emotions but the rewards are great. You become like your Father in Heaven.

SIMEON: THE DIMENSION OF JUDGMENT AND WISDOM

Simeon and Levi are brethren; instruments of cruelty are in their habitations. O my soul, come not thou into their secret; unto their assembly, mine honour, be not thou united: for in their anger they slew a man, and in their selfwill they digged down a wall. Cursed be their anger, for it was fierce; and their wrath, for it was cruel: I will divide them in Jacob, and scatter them in Israel. (Gen 49:5-7)

Let's deal with the Simeon dimension in the heavenlies. What is the meaning of his name? The direct meaning of the word is "heard." Simeon means to be heard. *Shema Israel Adonai Elohenu Adonai Echud.* "Hear, O Israel: The Lord our God is one Lord" (Deut 6:4).

Do you realize some people never actually see heaven? They hear more from heaven than they see into heaven. There are some people in church who do not feel. Now if you are not a feeler and you're in a Pentecostal church, you think God is not talking to you.

If you're not a seer and you do not see, then you think that you're really not seeing because you believe that the only way is to see in your imagination. The heaven you are open to usually has to do with the particular kind of relationship you have with God. In addition, there are some of you, even if God appeared to you in fire and brimstone, you would not see Him. Nevertheless, you would know He is there.

There is no reason for people to lie to themselves and say they are seeing what they do not see. It is happening a lot among some groups where people are lying about what they have seen. They do not see anything. They just want to be able to see because we have convinced them that it is the way you experience heaven. Those who don't have emotional goose bumps feel like something is wrong with them. There are many people who do not have real prophetic insight but every time they ask God for something, they get an answer. Every dimension of the 12 is a gateway into the other dimensions.

You work on the strengths that you already have and in the dimension you are in. There is a gateway there that will then transfer you to the other dimensions. You cannot operate out of Simeon if you are a Reuben. You cannot operate from Simeon as a way to get to Levi. You have to work in the dimension you are in and move up from there.

DEALING WITH YOUR EMOTIONS

The heaven of Simeon is where your emotions are. These emotions are not the 'feelings' discussed in Reuben. Emotions are not feelings. Emotions are embedded realities in your body that have potentialities. Your emotions also reflect things that are in God. God gets angry but not out of passion or out of feelings. God is love.

This is why marriages fail so much. It is because everybody thinks that love has to do with feelings, or love has to do with what the other

> **"** However, that is not love. That is just your feelings ruling you, which is okay. Just be clear with yourself what it really is. **"**

person does. Most of the feelings that you call love is not love. You do not love the way God loves. You love based on Eros. You love based on give and take. However, that is not love. That is just your feelings ruling you, which is okay. Just be clear with yourself what it really is.

One Sunday, after a service, someone asked me, "If your wife commits adultery, will you stay married to her?" I said, "yes." The person was shocked. Most people in Christianity and in America make a condition upon which they will love a person, then claim they love the person. It is a hard thing, but if you want to learn how to be like God, then you had better get ready. What you're saying you do and when you say you love you're talking about doing things for people because they're going to behave a certain way.

Even the husband or the wife you are married to - you're only married to them as long as they haven't done something that really hurts you. Your love for them is only there because of that. So, is your love based on an absolute principle, or is it based on your feelings? If your feelings are hurt, the marriage is over. It just depends on how hurt you are. Are we Christians really? Are we really trying to be like God? If you begin a relationship saying "These are the things you're going to do" and "my love for you will never end," - that is going to make the relationship end. You just have to admit you have no capacity for love - your love is based on yourself. So I am just saying, be honest. Let's all just be honest with ourselves. This is a great starting point for change.

The kind of love that God is asking for is too much for most of us. God says, love your enemies. What are your enemies trying to do? They are trying to kill you. They're trying to gouge out your eyes, cut off your ears, and put them in your mouth, and get you to eat your ears that they cut off. They're trying to poke you with all kinds of nails. They just killed your brothers and sisters and buried them, or brought their heads to you. They brought their tongues and put them on your table. This happens to Christians. The Bible says love your enemies. Do you think Jesus was trying to be namby-pamby? Most of the people you love are people who love you. You have never really loved your enemy. Nobody in the world has, otherwise we would not have wars.

Therefore, to move from Reuben to Simeon, you have to face your emotions because that is what Simeon is. Simeon is the one who, out of anger along with his brother, wiped out the whole village because they were offended at what was done to their sister. In the Reuben dimension, you are dealing with unstable feelings. This is the negative side of the judgment and the severity of Simeon.

In the Simeon dimension you're dealing with emotions that are actually embedded in the body. They are activated and are unable to be controlled - which is real instinctual rage. So deal with your feelings so you can deal directly with your emotions.

Know that emotions are more powerful than feelings - not the other way around. This is because emotions are embedded in your body. Feelings are the result of what happens to you but emotions are built in your body. So this is that heaven of judgment because they test your level of mature responses. This is good. It is a great place to be, but you cannot live there forever. It's judgment issues. However, you cannot be in judgment and be in love at the same time.

Here is a prayer based 1 Corinthians 13:

"I thank you Lord that your love in me endures long and is patient and kind. Your love in me is never envious, nor boils over with jealousy, is boastful, or vainglorious, and does not display itself haughtily. Your love in me is not conceited, arrogant, and inflated with pride. It is not rude, unmannerly, and does not act unbecomingly. Lord, your love in me, does not insist on its own rights or its own way for it is not self-seeking. Your love in me is not touchy or fretful or resentful. It takes no account of the evil done to it. It pays no attention to a suffered wrong. Your love in me does not rejoice at injustice and unrighteousness, but rejoices when right and truth prevail. Your love in me bears up under anything and everything that comes. It is ever ready to believe the best of every person. Its hopes are fadeless under all circumstances and it endures everything without weakening. Your love in me never fails, never fades out, or becomes obsolete or comes to an end."

When you deal with the first two dimensions that God wants to bring us into, it is all about experiencing purification and cleansing yourself. It is a heaven. You have a relationship with God.

When you get to this place, you are sensitive to every wrong done to you, but you are also sensitive to every wrong done to everybody else, and you think you are the caped crusader trying to fix everything.

That is where most of the liberals who claim to be Christians in America are, including a lot of the evangelicals. We want to judge everything. Just remember, he that lives by the sword shall die by the sword. If you spend your time living in judgment, somebody else will take you to court and judge you too. It is better to let go of a wrong.

The throne of God here in Simeon is on the waters and sits above the waters, getting ready for you to come under subjection. You come under subjection by subjecting yourself to the Word. The throne of God here is a seat of judgment. You can judge all you want but when you are in Reuben or when you are in Simeon, to love is hard because you are yet to deal with your feelings and emotions.

THE FIRMAMENT AND JUDGMENT

When people talk about the 'second heaven', where there are demons and other things, there is agitation because demonic powers are there. They are not really in the 'second heaven', they are in the firmament. The firmament is different in a sense. There's a distinction made in the Scriptures. Psalms 19:1 says "The heavens declare the glory of God; and the firmament showeth his handiwork." Genesis 1:16-17 says: "God made two great lights. He made the stars also. And God set them in the firmament of the heaven to give light upon the earth."

There's a distinction made between a firmament and heaven. The firmament is like a skin that covers the earth. What the demons do in the firmament is actually keep things from going into the heavenly dimension. So just like your flesh operates in the skin of your body, the same thing operates at that level. They operate using your feelings, especially the negative ones. In operating that way, they bring you under judgment. Therefore, when you are operating in judgment, you are operating in the second level heaven, but not the heaven of the heavens. There is also a throne a of judgment set up there.

Remember, there are different seats of judgment. There are seats of judgment that judge sin. There are seats of judgment that are seats of distribution where God distributes gifts and gives them to His children and says "Okay, this is yours. This is yours. This is yours. This is yours."

In a sense, it is where the will of the Father is read and things are given to the children. It is still a seat of judgment, but it's a different kind of throne. In the Scriptures, we call it the *Bema* seat where Christians are given their reward. This throne in Simeon is different. We are talking about taking vengeance here. It is your right to take vengeance, but love triumphs over judgment.

LEVI: THE DIMENSION OF PRIESTHOOD AND UNDERSTANDING

Simeon and Levi are brethren; instruments of cruelty are in their habitations. O my soul, come not thou into their secret; unto their assembly, mine honour, be not thou united: for in their anger they slew a man, and in their selfwill they digged down a wall. Cursed be their anger, for it was fierce; and their wrath, for it was cruel: I will divide them in Jacob, and scatter them in Israel. (Gen 49:5-7)

Simeon and Levi are twins but they are also separate. Levi gets to support Simeon because Levi is a being of two worlds. Remember that. Levi is a priest. A priest lives in two worlds. Every priest lives and connects to two worlds.

What does Levi mean? Let's start with what it literally means because it allows us to get an insight. One of the problems we have as Christians and as spiritual people, is we move into the spiritual realm when we haven't dealt with the actual meaning of something. It actually hurts us.

Levi means "joined." We are going to talk about the

mystical meaning later on. Levi means attachment. When you look at the literal meaning, then you understand that the principle that activates your heaven is the same principle that can hinder you from experiencing the other heavens. Let me give you an example.

Reuben means excited, excellent, dignity. These very qualities create hubris and he goes and sleeps with his father's wife. Simeon means "heard." Simeon is somebody that gets an answer, no matter what. Either he has been heard by God or he wants to be heard by any means necessary. I am going to be heard. I am going to get justice. It is going to happen whether you like it or not. Therefore he convinces his brother to kill a whole village in order to be heard.

Why does Levi join Simeon to go and kill? Because it is intrinsic in his nature. The way he experiences his own dimension is by joining other people. There are some of you who will never enter your heaven unless there is somebody you are working with. You cannot walk alone. If you get into a group where they are having experiences, you get the same experience because that's just your nature. When people are not around, you do not have the experience. It does not mean something is wrong with you. You ask, "How come when I'm at home I cannot experience that?" It is because that is not you. It is because you are operating in the Levi dimension.

When the land is divided in Israel, Simeon does not really get anything. He gets joined to Benjamin. Every time Simeon cries, somebody has got to come help him. You never see them going to war. You never see them succeeding in a lot of areas because everybody is coming to help them. Levi does not get anywhere either. Levi doesn't get anything because the only way he gets his inheritance is by attaching himself to other people. It is not a bad thing.

If you think about it from the way we look at life, you would think that is terrible. Nevertheless, the attachment, that joining of Levi, is what allows him to be able to join people with God. It is part of his character. It is part of how he functions as a priest.

ACCESSING THE HEAVENLIES

Before we move on let's discuss a facet of the heavenlies. There is a heavenly dimension that deals with water (Reuben). There is a heavenly dimension that deals mainly with the auditory where you just hear (Simeon). It is nothing but sound. You cannot see anything. It is sound. Some people go up and they listen. They hear music but they do not know where it's coming from. They do not see angels singing. I was in a meeting in Illinois and there was a young lady singing. When she stopped singing, the voices continued, and we could hear choirs singing. But only a few of us could hear it.

> " I was in a meeting in Illinois and there was a young lady singing. When she stopped singing, the voices continued, and we could hear choirs singing. But only a few of us could hear it. "

There is an angelic protocol for Reuben. The reason you were baptized in water was not just to bury you, but to activate the angelic principle of the firstborn. A Christian that is not baptized really misses this aspect. You must be baptized. It is not a suggestion. There are names for these angels. Angels are made of the four elements - water, air, fire, and matter (I did not say earth. It is not the kind of matter you think of).

If you have seen angels, some of them glow like gold. Some of them sparkle like diamonds. They look like glass. There are a few angels who are actually a combination of the four. Therefore, when we deal with Reuben, we're dealing with angels that are made mainly of liquid form, from the watery forms.

The reason most demonic forces that use sexuality are so strong in Africa and other places is because they are watery spirits. That is why you have water spirits and that is why all these sexuality issues come up. That is the weakness of Reuben.

> **"** This is why the name of God is so important in what we do - the vibrating of Yod Heh Vav Heh. **"**

When you move from your emotions, you must go through the place of being heard. This is Simeon. There is a dimension in heaven where, if you get in it, there's so much acoustic sound. Do you know everything in the world vibrates sound? In this place sound is so strong. This is why you need to develop your own sound - your own unique, personal sound that unlocks this area for you.

But here is the problem. Two things can happen to you in this realm. One of the things that can happen to you is you always want to be heard - even when you are not right. This means you begin to talk too much. You find yourself developing a spirit of offense when you think people are not hearing what you are saying. This is the weakness of Simeon.

This is why the name of God is so important in what we do - the vibrating of Yod Heh Vav Heh. If you develop your own personal sound then you can activate the various sounds at different levels. The sounds at this level are so infinite. When God came down upon Mt. Sinai the Bible says, "and Israel *saw* the sound." When you develop your personal sound (even though you cannot see it with your eyes) at a certain level you will begin to see the sounds themselves - but you must develop your personal sound. Part of the way you develop them is by calling upon the name of the Lord, using the name of Jesus Christ, proclaiming the word of the Lord - but saying it in such a way you hear it. It is your voice. Not somebody else's voice.

For Christo-centric meditations go to www.seraphcreative.org/dro

One of the best ways to do this is really to lock yourself up somewhere and just shout at the top of your lungs and do it for hours until you release your own personal sound. This is what happens when we do worship - people literally get free and start shouting and things happen. You need to develop your own unique sound. When you develop that sound, it unlocks a dimension for you.

There are dimensions in this place that when you release that sound that is yours and that is uniquely your own signature, then God releases in this dimension words that create things or beings that you need for a particular purpose. Everything I say here everybody can experience.

The key is you have to start from where your own particular strength is. Do not try to start from somewhere that is not your strength or you are going to be frustrated. Do not try to see if you are not a seer. You are going to be frustrated. But if you are a seer, start from there, and you will begin to hear, and you will begin to move in these dimensions. When you get into any room, in the level of Reuben for example, there is sound. But what is wrong, what happens?

The sounds are all emotional. They are all intrinsic. They are motions in the body. There is no distinction of voice. So you find yourself getting confused. You do not know what you are feeling because feelings do not really talk.

But if you are able to master that water, that sound, that emotion you begin to hear. Then you are able to transport from Reuben into Simeon and your ears become open.

The tribes are foundational from the perspective of the earth but the Apostles are foundational from the perspective of the heavens. The Apostles are connected to the person of the Messiah and serve as His immediate circle. When looking at the city from the heaven it is upside down so that apostolic is the grounded in heaven. Every foundation is also a gateway (just like every altar is a gateway). So just because you are working on one particular heaven does not mean the other heavens are closed to you. When the gateway of one is opened, you are able to transport from one place to the next. However, every dimension you go into, you need to work on. In addition, these gates are also interconnected with different parts of your body - different emotions, different aspects of your body.

We are using these as metaphors. God gave them to us so that we can use them as typologies and metaphors in order to explain what is up there? In this cubic heaven of the 24, which is the tribes and the apostles, there are gateways. Because the gateways move upward, they do not move downward. They move upwards and sideways. There are pathways that go downward. But believe me, if you are not trained, you do not want to go there. So you move from heaven to heaven.

FORGIVENESS

Back to Levi. Let's return to Genesis 49. "Simeon and Levi are brethren. Instruments of cruelty are in their habitation. O my soul, come not thou into their secret unto the assembly.

My honor be not thou united for in their anger they slew a man and in their self will they dig down a well. Cursed be their anger for it was

> ❝ When you master this Levi dimension of heaven you can hear things that are not allowed for human beings to hear. ❞

fierce, and their wrath for it was cruel. I will divide them in Jacob and scatter them in Israel."

In Deuteronomy 33, Moses, in order to allow Israel to traverse the supernatural realm without hindrance, moves Simeon and Levi out of the way. This is because both Simeon and Levi cause anger and bitterness. "Is there a heaven where you can actually experience bitterness?" Yes. What activates both anger and bitterness is unforgiveness. You cannot really master these two.

When you master this Levi dimension of heaven you can hear things that are not allowed for human beings to hear. You become an inheritance of God. You actually experience what it means to be possessed by God as an inheritance.

There are places you cannot go in heaven unless you have mastered this. That is why Moses shut them out and took them away. Israel was not ready to experience that dimension. This dimension of heaven you cannot experience unless you understand forgiveness.

I am going to give you an example of what I am talking about - when Jesus died on the cross. You could stay in the Reuben heaven and play with water and have angels do things for you, but you cannot be heard by God and understand the voices of that place. You cannot understand what it means to be joined with God and move into the dimension of connecting with God unless you forgive. Jesus could have never been reunited with the Father and experienced that heavenly realm unless He forgave from the cross.

In the Levi and the Simeon realm - the Simeon realm in particular - you need to work on your hearing capacity. Remember, Jesus said "Be careful *how* you hear." Not be careful not *what* you hear but Be careful *how* you hear - because this is a gateway. This is the only gateway that has no covering. It has no protection. It is the only gateway that goes directly into your head and into your heart. It is the only gateway that balances you. So be careful not *what* you hear but *how* you hear. What is it that can hinder you from actually hearing? Bitterness. Gall.

So, if you ever have an experience in the heavens and you get into a certain dimension and there are some noises that you can't stand - that has to do with your unforgiveness. You need to begin to release yourself because it is a sound that is coming based on what you are producing from inside of you. You cannot actually hear the voice of God very clearly. If you hear the voice of God, sometimes it is your own voice.

I am not trying to tell you that you are not seeing God, but you cannot actually get to the point where you begin to have that experience unless God is calling you up to come and experience something.

Now you have to go through it. The noise will almost kill you. You will just get so uncomfortable because there is something happening inside of you. You cannot cross to the next level. What is judged here is your heart. What is judged here are your feelings.

You have these angelic forces that are dealing with elements. They are elemental beings. This is where we have what is called 'coals of fire'. Coals of fire are also angelic beings

(I did not say flames of fire in this particular circumstance).

However, these are also enflamed by you. They become strengthened as you become strengthened. They become weak as you become weak - because they are intrinsically connected with you. You are going to see the words "coals of fire" in Scripture. Why did we say coals of fire? Because Levi deals with fire. Also, when Jacob talks about Simeon and Levi, he talks about their fierce anger, how it burned. It can be cleansed and become a fire that warms or it can become a fire that destroys.

Remember, I told you everything has two dimensions. There is always a negative and a positive. You cannot run away from it. Before you can experience the heaven you want to experience in this dimension, you need to deal with the negative side inside you. If you don't deal with the negative, you're not going to have manifestations in the material realm.

This is what happens. You get to heaven, and you have all this experience. Because you haven't dealt with yourself and you have not really dealt with the things that bother you, when you come down from heaven, these issues get captured in matter and then you can never do anything about them. If it is spiritual, they get eaten up by the time you get down here. They do not manifest in the material. They actually get eaten up by the material. They are two different things.

THE DISCIPLINE OF DEALING WITH YOURSELF

How do you hear? If I am talking to you, are you hearing yourself or are you hearing me? You think you are listening, but you are actually talking to yourself while I am talking to you. So who are you listening to - me or you? If God is talking to you and you are talking, who are you listening to? It is a discipline. Now we are going to talk about discipline. This is where God teaches you.

When you begin to move in these dimensions God begins to teach you how to actually be silent. Not just silent in terms of not talking but silent in terms of not thinking ahead of God. I began training myself on how to actually stop my thoughts. When I say this, people think I am joking. I can actually stop my thoughts for 10, 15 minutes and nothing is happening in my head. I trained myself.

The first way I began to do this was to focus on the back of my head and just focus on nothing back there. I did it for months and years. All of a sudden, it started happening. I would just stop and not think about anything. You can force yourself to do it. You need to start focusing. The best way to do this is to find a small dot in the back of your head and focus on it. Just focus on it.

Do not do anything else. Just focus on that dot. When you are able to do that, then you have a space to actually hear God. You can make a distinction between when you are hearing yourself and when you are hearing God. Most of the things you are hearing is yourself because if you were actually hearing God there would have been manifestations.

Sometimes God is talking to you but you are not making a clear distinction between what God is saying and what you are saying to yourself. In these dimensions, God trains you.

These heavenly dimensions you're going through are training grounds for you. Your Father is trying to train you about certain things so that you're able to receive and to manifest. You can deal with these heavenlies without being trained. Immediately you can walk in, but there are certain tests that come to you. They may not come while you are in the heavens, but they will come immediately when you come back down.

When you go up to the heavens, God's treating you well and you're hearing all this sound. Then you step back down and the first person you meet says something that grates on your nerve and you respond. That means you really didn't learn anything up there.

The only thing that will embed the experience of heaven in your body is somebody coming against you in that area. So if you get into the heavenlies and you have this great experience, when you start coming down, the first thing God allows is for somebody to go directly against that experience. If they don't go directly against that experience, it's never going to be written and carved into your soul. That's what scripture means by "we must through much tribulation enter into the kingdom of God (Acts 14:22)"

Do you know that many of you encounter angels every day - but you encounter them only in sounds. You don't see them all the time, but you hear them talking to you. You really can't make the distinction between an angel talking to you and your imagination because you're still trafficking with familiar spirits. So what happens in the Levi dimension is God begins to teach you to make a distinction between your wishful thinking, your anger, your complaints about people and this heavenly sound. Sometimes the way God will deal with you is He will put a particular sound in your soul and in your spirit and it keeps coming over and over again.

It could be the sound of music. If you cultivate it, listen to it and focus your whole attention, it will start drawing from the other realm into your being. It's happened to you. It might not even be Christian music but you hear the rhythm and the sound and something begins happening in your soul.

Because you don't realize what's happening, you think "Oh, it's just music." If you listen to the sound carefully enough and allow your soul to ride on the sound, you can actually begin to receive from the other realm - like visions and glorious things that are happening in the heavens.

PRIESTS MUST DEAL WITH THEIR ISSUES

> " He conjured up the face of the fallen cherubim from hell. "

God decides to inscribe His name on a piece of rock. He gives it to Moses - the two tablets. As Moses is coming down, he hears this sound. The people said to Aaron: "Aaron, do you realize that we don't know what happened to this guy Moses? And we want to join with you. We really want to. We feel connected to you. We feel you, Aaron. We know you feel us. So why don't you make us a god that will take us back to Egypt or take us into the promised land? As far as this man Moses, we don't know what happened to him."

And Aaron, being a Levite, joined with them. The first thing he does is he tells everybody to "Bring your gold; bring all your gold, every piece of gold you have, bring it to me." They bring it to him and the Bible says he cast it into a golden cow - a calf.

When Moses comes down he says to Aaron, "What have these people done to you? Do you hate these people that much that you have made them commit such a sin?" Aaron says, "My lord, you know these people. They're so stiff-necked." He doesn't talk about himself. He says: "They said to me, 'make us a god that will take us back to Egypt ... but Moses, we don't know what has happened to him. So I took their earrings and their gold, and I cast it into the fire and out came this calf."

You might laugh when he says that, but you have missed something. Remember, Aaron was the prophet of Moses and he was the selected high priest, before even he knew it. So he did what he did because of his attachment to God and his attachment to the people, but he was also attached to the other side, the negative side. So when he throws this gold into the fire, he literally calls up the calf from hell.

He said, "I cast it and out came the calf." He conjured up the face of the fallen cherubim from hell. Why else would the Bible say, "out came the calf"? This is what was written and you need to read what's written there. The Bible also says that Moses came down, and he heard the people screaming and writhing like snakes.

The people were literally possessed and their genetic structure was changing. So Moses asks, "Who is on the Lord's side?" and he says,

> **"** The people were literally possessed and their genetic structure was changing. **"**

"every man kill his brother, his mother, his sister, his father." Why? Because there was a genetic mutation caused by this calling up of the face of the fallen cherubim.

The cow is one of the faces of the cherubim. That's why you have people around the world worshiping the cow. So Aaron calls this fallen cherub up and Moses grinds the golden calf to powder and makes the people drink it as an antidote to what is happening to them.

When you are operating in this Levi heaven, this is where

you meet cherubim for the first time. Not everybody gets to meet cherubim. Only when you begin to enter this dimension do you begin to meet cherubim. But your blessedness is where you have been washed by the blood of Jesus Christ, so we don't have to face a lot of the other kinds of issues.

This is why you need the blood of Jesus Christ. This is why you need the name of Jesus - to keep you from doing exactly what Aaron did. There is no other human being, whose blood is that innocent and that pure, who can keep those things from coming out of hell. If you're operating in a dimension and you don't have Jesus Christ and you don't understand His blood, you're going to release things that are going to destroy you - unless God is merciful on you and pulls you out.

The cherubim have 4 faces - the face of a cow/ox, the face of an eagle, the face of a man, and the face of a lion. When the covering cherub fell, what God did was scatter His face among the four corners of the earth. And it's easy to see.

Most cultures worship either man, or a cat/lion, or a calf - it may be an elephant or a horse, but it's still a cow/ox. Some people worship and they use serpents, but they don't directly worship serpents. There are four faces, and God scattered them across the globe - across the universe actually. It was serious when Aaron called that face up. That's why, when you read the text, you may even laugh and say, Aaron just made up a story, but Moses took him seriously and started killing everyone who participated in it.

What is going to happen and what you see in the Book of Revelation is the constant attempt of human beings to bring the four faces of the cherubim together. That's what the antichrist, the beast and his prophets try to do - they try to bring the faces together. All witchcraft is geared towards trying to bring those four faces together. Only man can do that.

All the things that comes out of the sea in the Book of Revelation is because man calls them out from the sea. It's man that calls those things forth. Man is the one that's going to call out the creatures and issues that are going to destroy him. They're going to attack and do things to us. They don't have power to come on their own. If you are involved in witchcraft, you are part of the people empowering negativity and darkness.

In this Levi dimension you're going to have experiences and this is where your temptation to get into witchcraft comes. If you have not been tested in this area, you don't know anything about what you think you know. Every true priest who comes to the consciousness of their priesthood goes through this. You go through this because it is part of the cleansing process, where you cast out the negative attachments in order to hold to the true priesthood.

The priesthood of Melchizedek is different from that of Aaron because Aaron called up the calf from hell. We don't find Melchizedek doing one ritual. People who do rituals can get to this place. They can see into this Levi dimensions. When you, the Christian, have dealt with your issues, there is no longer the use of ritual to actually enter.

Now most of us don't like to deal with issues like this. We think, "I'm a Christian now; I don't have to struggle with that." Don't you know that is what happened to Jesus when he first was in the desert? Satan went to Him thinking, "Let's see if you will do the same thing." If Jesus had turned the stone into bread, where would the bread have come from? From Heaven or hell? If you listen to Satan you pull from that which is below. This is why it is so important to train yourself to hear

God. Only then will you be able to tell the difference.

PASSING THE TEST

Let's structure it now. In this level, God begins to assign cherubim. When I decided to start going into heaven again, one of the reasons I stopped trying to deal with the things in the supernatural was because of the kinds of experiences I was having in my basement in Illinois. I was spending 8 hours a day in prayer. I had seen things but then I finally got into this Levi realm.

Now seeing things is different from actually being there. You can see the heavenlies, but it's different from actually being there. I was praying in my room and all of a sudden the walls disappeared into the basement. Flames of fire were all over and here comes this being and every cell in my body was scared. It was just turning. It was a cherubim.

It said to me, "If you will agree to partner with me and to serve me..." (See, that's a red flag right there) "... If you want members in your church and crowds who will follow you, and money and fame. No matter what you do, you will still succeed." I said, "I just have one question. Did Jesus send you? Do you know Jesus?" Man, the sound and the shriek in that room! I felt like my body was going to tear apart. He said, "I will show you and I will teach you a lesson you will never forget." I won't tell you what happened after that but all hell broke loose.

Now you need to understand the Lord didn't come to help me - because he wasn't the Lord's test. God's been training me and teaching me. So the cherubim left angry and things started happening. I know God protected me but God didn't come to me physically as He usually comes.

When I started studying, the Lord would walk into my room. For three years, the Lord Jesus Christ would come in my room and start teaching me the Scriptures but He never talked about this situation. Until today, the Lord has not talked to me about it because it's not His to deal with - it's my issues that are in my DNA from my lineage as a Cohen. Do you get what I just said? There are certain things you just have to go through but when you get to this place, this Levi dimension, it's a dimension where you are joining with people and interceding for them.

INTERCESSION

Levi is the dimension of intercession. Intercession is not about fighting with the devil. That's what most of us think intercession is - binding the devil, fighting with the devil, wrestling with the devil, throwing him on the ground and doing World Wrestling Federation on him. That's not what it is. Intercession is standing in for somebody else. That's what it is. Standing in the gap. An intercessor is not standing in the gap between the person and the devil. He or she is standing in the gap between a human being and God. So all that activity you're doing - screaming and shouting at the devil - you're not interceding for anybody because intercession has to do with standing in for your brother or sister in front of God.

That's the difference. There are other things you can do when dealing with the devil, but that's not intercession. Intercession is standing in the presence of God and pleading on behalf of your brother, saying, "My brother Joe is just dumb but I still love him. Lord, don't allow him to be destroyed." I'm saying it in a way that sounds funny, but that's simply what intercession is. "Instead, Lord, I stand here. If you want to do it, do it to me."

Most of us don't even intercede to that extent - we deflect the stuff to the devil and refuse to take responsible as sons. If you're interceding, you're the one in the middle and you get to bear the burden of the people. Once you are able to get into this place, you find yourself carrying other people's burdens. The reason only Aaron could call up the calf was because Levi is the burden bearer of the people.

In this Levi dimension you carry burdens - if you have been a Christian for a while, there was a time in your life when you just could feel people's burdens. It was like, "Lord, why do I have to carry all this burden for these people?" You were so burdened for people and you carried that burden.

You were operating in the Levi dimension of heaven. You were standing for people, you were crying for people, you were burdened for them. Now if you are not careful, if you have not dealt with this witchy issue, you're going to have a problem. You're going to want people to acknowledge you - that you are the "master" who delivered them. "If I was not interceding for you, you wouldn't have been able to overcome your problems".

This is control and manipulation because then you start getting into ritual. Most people in this area - and those who are involved in Kabbalah - are involved in this control. They want to use ritual to control elements. They have not been delivered from this need in their life. Many people in our Pentecostal context do the same thing. They use prophetic words to manipulate people because they have not yet dealt with this.

There's a test here, in the Levi dimension. You must learn how to hear. You must watch what you join yourself to.

NAVIGATING THE FIRST TRIAD

It's an ascending order. Reuben, then Simeon, then Levi. When you get to the Levi dimension, there is a formation that happens. You have completed a cycle and now you are a priest. You're able to stand for other people because you have dealt with that inside of you that says, "hear me." You have dealt with one aspect.

You're dealing with your feeling aspect, your feeling centers. All that's in you that makes you form attachment. It's where you do actions just because it feels good. You like it. This is where you go into heaven and you see gold and you see silver. You like it so much but you never manifest anything on earth because it's all about you.

When you deal with this and you become a real priest (because you have dealt with a lot of issues and you're not attached to them) then you're able to begin to walk in manifestation. There is a jump that happens into the next level. You have the water, you have the coals of fire (remember, I didn't say flames of fire) and you have the smoke. It is smoke and flame because it is the smoke of sacrifice of yourself. And they're all ephemeral - they're things that are illusionary.

TRUE TRANSFORMATION

There is a ladder of movement. Begin with Reuben, then

you go to Simeon, then you go to Levi. When you come to Levi there is a strong transformation because priests can take over other people's lives and make them do crazy things. Most of the guys you see in the occult are people who have diverted their priestly gift to the other way.

In this dimension, your feelings become more purified and more subtle. We're dealing with emotions now. You have worked on the centers of your emotions and now you no longer react in Anger. This heaven allows you to deal with all kinds of issues as God is training you. If you're not trained in these three levels you're going to see a lot of things but you won't manifest it. I keep talking about manifestation because we are in a period where God wants to manifest things but most Christians can not.

How much manifestation are you seeing? You see feathers falling from the sky - so what? I don't think that's important. I don't think gold dust is important. I think what's important is self-transformation - when you're transformed, your feelings are transmuted in Reuben, your emotions are transmuted in Simeon and your priestly instincts are transmuted in Levi to actual priesthood, then you are not trying to control the "small stuff" - you actually impact the Elijah sphere (Sphere of Judgment and Transformation). That sphere of what seems to be the inevitability of judgment can be supervened by the true priests who knows how to intercede from the heavens.

I'm talking about terra formation, physically changing creation, when I'm talking about the church. Whatever you terra form, you do so in your own image. If we're having to deal with the old us (all this nonsense that we have in ourselves and the damage that is in you and me) then we are still asleep - and what we create will contain these issues?

This is the level that deals with elemental spirits. All of this has to do with magic - elemental spirits. It is here that you begin the formation of the cherubic – the primary cherubic formation. The cherubim are really the foundational angels of God because they carry the four faces of God (Lion-Ox-Eagle-Man) and the four dimensional name of God (Yod-Hey-Vav-Hey). Moreover, the covering cherub that fell were supposed to cover not only the throne of God but also man.

In the Book of Ezekiel, the angel that fell was supposed to cover the throne. Covering the throne also meant covering humanity - because humanity is a throne of God. Humanity is a dwelling place of God. So here you begin the cherubic formation. The reason God gave the priesthood to Israel was to continue the cherubic formation, in which cherubim are kept in their positions, the fallen cherubim are kept away, and the upper cherubim are released. And may I say, if you can receive it, that new cherubic principles are created.

Let's look at what a cherubim is. A cherubim has four faces. The first three faces are elemental. First, you're dealing with a cow/ox in your fallen nature, and the second face you're dealing with the lion (not the concept of the lion as Jesus Christ). With the face of the eagle, you're dealing with the ego because it has a capacity to take flight and to move to the next dimension.

When you overcome the fallen nature in you of these three angelic principles, then man comes to the fold. All of these three elemental things work by instinct. They don't think. They just react. The cow reacts, it does not think. What makes the cherubim powerful is the DNA of man that God puts in the cherubim. So the cherubim have a human face because it is man-powered. There are four faces and in the center, right in the cherubim, is another human being - son of man (not 'The Son of Man').

So the flight of the eagle releases the imagination and the intellectual nature of man that allows him to begin his operation in his divine nature. Most human beings operate out of the cow or lion. The point is that most of the time, you're not operating in the eagle. You are eating, sleeping, drinking as a cow. Flight is not really an option. Very few people are actually rational and act beyond eating and sleeping.

So you need angels that give you food and angels that let you lounge under a tree and open your mouth. To fly is not easy. Most people who are flying are like the eagle, whose main purpose for flying is to look down for something to eat but that dimension is where the work for your next level takes place - to become a human being, to become a man - Anthropos - to become Adam. It's when your imagination begins to take flight.

ENGAGING YOUR FEELINGS

Before you can do that, you have to deal with all of the elemental issues. You need to deal with those feelings by engaging them. Engage them - not act on them. Engaging does not mean to go do them. Engaging means feeling them and asking yourself questions: "I feel like this now. Why do I feel like this? What is wrong with you? What is this? Eww, that's gross. Why are you being so gross?" You are talking to yourself.

Let's say you're a man and every woman you see, all your body stands up. You're asking yourself, "What's wrong with me? Why is this happening to me? What is going on? Why do I feel the way I feel? What is the difference between this woman and that woman?" The more you think about it, the more you realize there is no difference. There is something happening in you.

There is something in your DNA that is making this happen. It is the same thing with women: "Why am I angry over here and not angry over there? What's up?" You want that car and you think you should be the one to have the car? Good for you. You want the car. What is it about that car and you? What is the connection? What would you do if you had an opportunity to take that car away from that guy?

Then you start giving yourself an excuse - I would never do that kind of thing. However, you know what will happen. You may not kill the guy to take the car, but if you had to cheat him out of it, you would cheat him out of it. Then you would say, "God blessed me."

If you had $50,000 right now, you would go buy the car. You have not stolen it, but you are a thief because you coveted it from the person. You have to deal with yourself because you feel "I want that car and I want it now." What is wrong? Why do I want it? What makes me want it so badly that I am willing to rob myself of $50,000 in the bank that can help me do greater things than to buy it? It is not true that the only sin in the church is sex.

Ask yourself questions and you will notice what you feel and why. When you think "I want that necklace. I want it." ask yourself which "I" wants the necklace? Is it the cow "I," or the lion "I," or the eagle "I"? On the other hand, is it the human "I"? Which one? Who really wants it? Is it the "I" of your friends who want the necklace because they are also an "I" inside of you. Is it the "I" of your parents who would love to see you have a nice necklace or have a nice car? Is it the "I" of your wife, or your spouse? Which "I" is it? This heaven is where you work on your feelings and emotions and thoughts.

This is the heaven that you see. For 90% of us, the heaven we see is this one. This is why we spend so much time in warfare. We have to kill things. We have to kill serpents. We have to kill a black tiger. It is YOU! Moreover, the dragon, with all the jewels in it, is you. It is an "I" that you created. You projected it out there and it is fighting you. When you kill it, you kill off that part of yourself until you become unified.

However, you cannot be unified in your singular soul, which was created to bear the image of God, unless you are unified in your feelings, your emotions and your thoughts. Remember, I did not say, "Go do it." I said, "*engage* it." Do not let it run, and do not deny it. Do not think, "Oh, that's not me. That is not my emotion. It is not happening to me. I am too pure and too holy. I'm too righteous."

It will keep happening until you engage it. You have to call it out, front and center. This is where you do the heavenly court procedures. You put it in front of you and you say, "Sit. Sit in front of me. I want to talk to you. Cow! Look up from eating the grass. Lion! Wake up from under the shade and let me talk to you."

Therefore, when we have overcome this, we deal with the unthinking feelings, which are simple instincts. This is what actually releases the flesh - because we are not thinking when we do this. Then we deal with the feelings that are given to us for a purpose. They are not terrible. They are not bad. It is just that you have to tune them and experience them purposefully. Remember, feelings are not emotions. That is where the catch comes, because you think your feelings are emotions.

Feelings are the result of you talking up/out your emotions. Feelings are the effects. You know that you can be angry about something without feeling anything. What makes your feelings rise up and become uncontrollable? Unless you are sick and you're just not balanced, most feelings are the result of self-talk. That is why it is so important you to learn how to talk.

It is true that when I pinch my friend hard, he is going to feel pain. However, it is not really the pain that makes him upset. If he is walking and hits his hand, he is going to shake it off. He's not going to get angry. What happens when I pinch him? What does he do? He does more than think. He reacts and self-talks from the reaction. He may get the same kind of reaction that he does from hitting his hand. This hurts! Then he begins to say to himself, "He pinched me! Why did he pinch me? He pinched me!" Does his anger - the feeling he gets - really come from thinking or do they come from agitating and whipping up his emotions?

If he actually thought about it, he probably would not be as upset as he is. In addition, if he is upset, he is not making a choice about whether he is going to be upset or not. So is he really thinking? Most of the time, when you think you are thinking, you're not thinking - you are just reacting. It is the same thing with all of us.

Thinking assumes consciousness. What is consciousness? Consciousness is grounded in the will, so anything you don't do from your deliberate will, you are not conscious of.

So what is God working on in these heavenly dimensions of Reuben, Simeon and Levi? What is God working on in these three heavenly dimensions? It is your will. His intent is to unify your will. "Your will be done on earth, as it is in heaven." The earth is you.

BECOMING FREE TO CHOOSE

You are dealing with your fallen nature. It is warped until the new Adam/last Adam/true Adam is developed. Many of the things you and I do, we do based on assumptions and based on external factors. We do them based on our education and what people have told us we ought to do. We do them because religion tells us we ought to do them. I am not going

> **"** It is your will. His intent is to unify your will. "Your will be done on earth, as it is in heaven." The earth is you. **"**

to protect any sacred cows here. You do them because God tells us to do them. Good for you. However, what do you do because you choose to do it?

You became a Christian because you were scared to go to hell. Alternatively, you became a Christian because you do not want God to become upset with you or you want something from God. It is okay, it's not bad. It is neither wrong nor right. It is just that you have to ask yourself, "If I became a Christian based on all of that, am I free?" You have to come to the point where you choose God purely because you choose God. You do not choose God based on anything else.

Usually when you choose God based on these things - on this grass-eating, lazy, shadow-dwelling, high-flying, eye focused on meat principle - what happens? When you cannot find the meat from your height, you fall to the ground. When the shadow is gone, you become like Jonah and get angry with God. When you cannot find good grass, you kick.

The person we can use as an example is Job - the beginning of Job and the end of Job (Job was being like all of us in the middle). In the beginning when everything bad happened, Job said, "the LORD gave, and the LORD hath taken away; blessed be the name of the LORD" (Job 1:21)

He said things like, "Shall we receive good from the hand of the Lord and not evil?" Then the adversity came. What was God doing with Job? It was so that Job would choose God for God. Not because it was comfortable. He made the choice. We also make that choice knowing God may actually fail us based on our expectations. It is hard.

Look at the three Hebrew children: Shedrach, Meshach, and Abednego in Daniel 3:17-18. They said to Nebuchadnezzar: "O king, we want to make something clear to you. The God that we serve, He is able to deliver us. But we want you to know something, that even if you do not deliver us, we are not going to serve your god. We're not going to bow before this."

Most people who claim to be Christians are not. They are just Christians because it is something good to do, something they think is nice. It is when trials really come that you discover who is a Christian. Because the only proof of your will is suffering. It is hard.

Your ability to choose chocolate versus vanilla does not prove you have a will. Your being able to choose among beautiful women who's going to be your wife doesn't prove you have a will. It just proves you have a sex drive.

The problem is we are not real. Eighty percent of people who are Christians are so because they want to go to 'heaven'. Good for you! You are going to go to heaven. However, you really have not made a willful choice because most of us are never going to be tested in our Christianity. Now please do not tell me your friends were calling you names when you were small, so that is how you know you made a choice. Don't tell me your co-workers will not let you go to lunch with them because you are a Christian. That is not suffering. You have to make a choice.

A story told by many preachers is where armed robbers came to rob the bank and they said, "We are only robbing Christians and the only people we are going to shoot are Christians." Only one woman in the whole of the bank says, "I'm a Christian." The rest of them were not Christians at that moment. The armed robbers took the lady out. They turned to the rest of them and said, "Sorry, you guys are not Christians. She is the only Christian. We did not come here to rob you. We came here to give some gold to somebody." Now if the robbers came in and said, "We got gold. How many Christians are here?" people would raise four hands! It sounds silly but it's true.

TRIALS REVEAL YOUR PROGRESS

Do you realize that if we are tested as being Christians most of us will fail. In fact, we do fail every day in the little things that are tested. That is why God wants you to develop a will. The only way I can actually prove that I love you is that I still want to hang around you - even if you do all kinds of things that you're not supposed to do to me. When you are in need, I still come to meet your need.

Somebody that we call our Master said "If you love those who love you, what credit is that to you? For even sinners love those who love them. "If you do good to those who do good to you, what credit is that to you? For even sinners do the same" (Luke 6:32-33 NAS). It is normal. If you love your wife and your children, does that make you a loving person? No, it makes you normal, but you are still a sinner just like all of us. Selfish, self-centered - you love what loves you.

Now, what if your neighbor gets up in the morning and says, "Damn you!", uses four-letter words and says all kinds of hateful things about you? If you say, "Good morning, my brother. God bless you." then maybe you understand a little bit of what I am talking about. It is not that difficult to not fight back, however you are considered a coward. What does it mean to be a Christian? You do not talk back when people say all kinds of things about you. Instead you remain quiet and everybody assumes that you must be a terrible person because people are talking about you. I observed that quality in somebody that we say we follow. His name is Jesus. That is whom we say we follow.

I like these heavens because the streets there are not paved with gold. It is trial by fire. Trial by water, by fire, by uplifting, by looking from the top down. It's a kind of trial but it's still heaven. Why do I say there is heaven in this? Because in this region of Reuben, Simeon and Levi, heaven is what you make it inside yourself. You tune it. This can be hell for you or it can be heaven for you.

Without going through this, you cannot get into the other heavens and have the kind of experience that John is having in the Book of Revelation, where he is seeing all these angels and seeing all these wonderful things. What you are not asking is, "How did John get to the point where he had all of this experience?" His whole life was the testing of these three dimensions.

John was a close friend of Jesus. He walked with Jesus. He and his brother , James, were like Levi and Simeon. In Luke 9 they said, "Let's bring down fire and burn up these Samaritans - these half casts and who are not in covenant with us! Let's kill them because they rejected the Master!" We are dealing with Simeon and Levi. However, John lives longer than his brother does and God purifies him until he is able to love. He is an attacher. He joins himself to Jesus. First, he is the one that wants to kill off everybody. Then the joining allows him to be attached to God.

When he overcomes these fallen issues, he becomes the one that talks about love and teaches love more than anybody else. He is the same guy that wanted to kill everybody off. He did not progress without a test.

Peter did not become the leader and the firstborn of the apostles without going through a test. He failed his test. Just because you fail does not mean it's the end (as long as you don't do what Judas did). Your failure is not supposed to be the end. Your failure is supposed to be a way of getting up and trying again until you tune it. Every failure in the process of attempting is a success.

These are the first three heavens. In 2 Corinthians 12 Paul says, "I went to the heavens. I went to the third heaven ... and I *heard*...." This is where you hear sound. Remember, there is a sound here. Paul also says he saw a lot of things, but it was not even lawful for him to say. This is where - when you begin to get into this dimension, when you begin to become, and you fly and you become man - you begin to hear sounds and the sounds begin to make sense.

In progressing through these first 3 dimensions God begins to reveal secrets to you. This is where God teaches you how to keep secrets. I understand Christians do not like the term "secrets." Christians get offended by the idea of secrets. They think there are no secrets. That is why they can blabbermouth. You tell them something and they just blabber.

A Christian hears something, he doesn't understand what it is, but he starts teaching it. This is where God teaches you how to keep secrets. In dealing with your issues in these dimensions He humbles you enough so that your mouth is not always open, like a leaky pump pouring out everything you hear. Do you realize what I am teaching you here? I have known some revelation for years but I would not talk about it because, to most people, it wouldn't make sense. I do not talk about it because I know most people are not going to believe it. If they do not read it in a book somewhere, it is not real to them.

Progressing through this first triad of Reuben, Simeon and Levi forces you to deal with your elemental issues. Your feelings and emotions. It can be a difficult thing, facing up and owning your true self. However it qualifies you for great things, to hear and judge clearly and to experience the secrets of God. Not many Christians make this journey through the first triad. They remain asleep.

What you do with this understanding is your choice. You are free to choose and there is no wrong answer - just the option of staying asleep, or waking up and going higher!

TRANSITIONING BETWEEN THE TRIADS
THROUGH THE SEVEN SPIRITS OF GOD

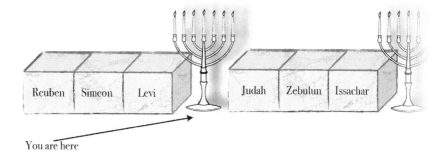

You are here

We started with the three heavens Reuben, Simeon and Levi. Every heaven has a gate that allows you, when you deal with it, to transition into the next one. From the first three heavens you take a quantum leap to Judah, Zebulun and Issachar. The leap is quantum. You pass through the Seven Spirits of God. You must pass through the menorah. These are flames of fire. That is why Levi ends with fire. He is the sacrifice. Levi is the person that deals with the sacrifice and the fire. The flames are here and these are purifying flames.

These are the Seven Spirits of God as described in Isaiah 11:2 "And the spirit of the LORD shall rest upon him, the spirit of wisdom and understanding, the spirit of counsel and might, the spirit of knowledge and of the fear of the LORD" and Revelation 1:4. Every time you transition you must deal with them.

In this place, you are dealing mostly with your flesh. Your flesh is tied to your body. It is connected to your emotions and feelings. When you deal with Reuben and with the issues that we have been talking about, you also deal with Simeon and that underlying spirit of offense.

That is what anger is. It is based on a spirit of offense. We are working from Genesis 49 (Jacob blessing his sons) and Deuteronomy 33 (Moses blessing the tribes) and Revelation (the tribes as revealed in the New Jerusalem). Remember, we have the 12 dimensions. This is your progression. We have looked at the first triad, which is the first of 4 triads. So we have the 3, the 4 and the 12 working together.

ELIJAH AND ELISHA

An example of the issues we are dealing with is in 1 Kings 19, about Elijah and Elisha. Elijah is told he is going to anoint three people (The symbols are all over Scripture). He is going to anoint Hazael of Syria; Jehu, son of Nimshiand and; Elisha, son of Shephat. Therefore, Elijah sends a person to go to Hazael's kingdom and anoint Hazael. He goes, anoints Hazael and runs away. The people said, "What did that guy come to do?" They said, "Oh, he's just a crazy fellow. He just came here." Then Hazael becomes king.

Elijah goes and anoints Jehu and he rides in and destroys Jezebel and all the people. Then he is ready to anoint Elisha because Elisha has been serving him. Elisha had already gone back home to farm. When he goes to Elisha, Elisha is plowing with 12 'yoke' or 'teams' or 'pair' of oxen. Therefore, there are 24 oxen. You are now dealing with a person, Elisha, who has trained himself to navigate the 24 dimensions, the Upper and the Lower dimensions. The 24 are there for a reason. It was a symbolic manifestation of tilling the ground by the heavenly conjunctions. It is in your Bible.

This helps to understand why Elisha had twice the miracles that Elijah had. Elijah went up to heaven but he was not able to combine the heavenly and the earthly. Just because you do miracles does not mean you understand the heavenly realm.

The problem we have with Elisha is that he had not dealt with his Reuben and Simeon issues. Therefore, even though he did all those miracles, he left no prodigy or legacy. Elijah left Elisha but Elisha left no-one. Remember, the sons of the prophet were not Elisha's children; they were Elijah's children (2 Kings 2:15).

People loved Elisha for his miracles but nobody wanted to relate to him because he would kill you if you make a mistake. It is in the Scripture. Kids would just say, "Go up, bald man." In response, Elisha says, "kill them." That tells you that he has not walked through his Reuben and Simeon issues (2 Kings 2:23).

The thing is, if you do not work through these issues, they are going to pursue you and follow you throughout your life. It won't stop you from experiencing the other dimensions, but you're not going to enjoy the fullness of those dimensions.

So let us say that in the coming months there is a big move of God and we are still dealing with issues way over back in Reuben. Is there any way for us to get over to a more mature heaven to receive it?

When the Father pours things out, everybody has a vessel big enough to receive what it is. However, you need to get yourself ready. You still have to work through your issues. When it is poured out, your level of maturity is what is going to determine how much you can actually pull from the realms of heaven into the material realm - but you are still going to receive. Remember you are born again. When the blessing flows through the Lord Jesus Christ, it comes to the Body. Each person receives according to the measure of grace given to him or her.

Just because you are having a problem in the Reuben dimension, for example, does not mean you will not receive. Reuben still receives. Simeon still receives an inheritance. Levi still deals with the sacrifice. However, the point is you must still overcome what it is you are supposed to overcome.

I preached one of my first messages in 1969. There is no way that God could have called me because of my righteousness because I was a kid. I understand what grace is! God can still use you. In terms of the development of your inner personality, of who you are, you have still got to go through a process.

If you are an angry person, you may tell me that God has taken away your anger. (This is something many Christians like to say, "God has taken away my anger.") What happens if immediately after you say that, God sends somebody into your life to make you angry? Then what do you do? You go back and say, "I'm so sorry. I thought I had overcome it." However, this is God's way of constantly working until your character is formed. Your character formation has to do with what you are going to produce in the future.

It's about the fullness of your destiny. God is working to manifest more of the fullness of your destiny through you so that, at a certain point, God doesn't have to constantly sovereignly do things. You have now developed into a son who can actually create on your own.

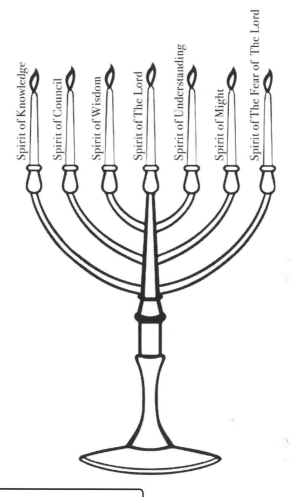

The seven candles are labelled, from left to right: Spirit of Knowledge, Spirit of Council, Spirit of Wisdom, Spirit of The Lord, Spirit of Understanding, Spirit of Might, Spirit of The Fear of The Lord.

THE SEVEN SPIRITS OF GOD

TRANSITIONING BETWEEN THE TRIADS

When we transition we need to deal with the issues at every juncture. The test of the quantum leap is how you deal with the Seven Spirits of God. Let's look at Isaiah 11:2 again. Here it names the Seven Spirits of God; *The Spirit of the Lord, wisdom, understanding, counsel, might, knowledge, and the fear of the Lord.* You have to deal with each of these spirits individually. Many people have a lot dealt with but they miss one aspect. The one that people miss most is the Spirit of Understanding or the Spirit of the Fear of the Lord.

It is these 7 spirits that act as "governors and tutors" to test whether you are ready to actually move. They may let you move to the next place but you are going to go in limping. For example, Jacob was leaving the house of Laban. The transition at the brook is the movement from the water, wrestling with an angel of fire, to be tested for the transition.

Jacob didn't try to deceive his brother. Jacob didn't try to do exactly what he did before. There is always a test to see if you have actually mastered your issues. The things you have not mastered in the past will make the test keep arising. Hubris is always your Achilles heel, chasing you.

If you watch the lives of all the people in Scripture, they had to go through these kinds of issues and be tested by the 7 spirits at every juncture. Remember, I told you about the judgment seats that are sitting here. Those are the thrones, and there are also seats - e.g. the mercy seat functions but is never referred to as a throne. However, it is the 7 spirits of the Lord who are testing your character.

ENGAGING THE SEVEN SPIRITS OF GOD

People ask me how do I engage the Seven Spirits of God in my life and in order to make this quantum leap from one set of triads to the next.

My answer is "acquire knowledge". Learn something new every day. Really learn. Do not just read. Learn. The Bible says get knowledge, get understanding, get wisdom. This is for a purpose. You should learn a simple practical application every day. More people with an education have been used by God than not. Remember that. And they are used at a higher level. Knowledge is the basis of revelation.

If not, a wise God would not have chosen Moses, a wise God would not have chosen Paul, a wise God would not have chosen Isaiah or a wise God would not have chosen Ezekiel. Ezekiel was not just a priest. He was a scientist. We need to stop thinking that ignorance, of itself, makes you a candidate for revelation. It does not.

One of the ways to engage the Spirit of the Lord is to acquire knowledge. That is why the Christian religion and the Jewish religion is the religion of books. God engaged Israel through writing.

Do not just read, however. Learn something that you can produce. The Spirit of the Lord will engage you. When you try to invent something, look for things that need to be solved and engage your mind. First, the Spirit of Wisdom will engage you if you want to create a solution to a problem or if you want to create something or craft something. In any business the way to do it is to say, "This is what I want to create. I want to create a straw that allows people to suck water from two miles away."

I am being humorous but you know what I'm talking about. Nobody has ever done it. Give the Holy Spirit something to work with. Your job is to find where there are problems and then try to create the solution. There is nothing so powerful that draws the Spirit of Wisdom as where a solution is needed.

Do not engage the Spirit of Wisdom just by going up to heaven, kissing her and falling at her feet. Remember, the

Bible says by wisdom the Lord created the heavens and the earth (Prov 3:19, Jer 10:12 and 51:15). When you come into a place where creativity is needed, and you truly desire to create a solution to a problem, the Spirit of Wisdom will engage you. The Spirit of Wisdom does not just engage Christians. She engages all people who are looking for solutions to problems (James 1:5). So what problem are you trying to solve? Maybe it is relational. It doesn't have to be scientific. Wisdom is about a practical solution to a practical problem.

The Spirit of Knowledge is about information. However, it is also about interacting with what has already been created to find out how it is done. Nature is one of the greatest ways to learn about God. Study the sun. Study the moon, stars, wind, flowers and human beings. Observe. Study yourself. Learn how your emotions work.

Engage the Spirit of Knowledge but remember, knowledge is an abyss. There is no end to knowledge. Knowledge will come. The more you seek information, the more knowledge comes. However, getting knowledge is one thing and getting understanding is another. Knowledge comes with information. But understanding comes by being. A problem we have in the West is that we separate knowledge from being. That is why we praise people who know a lot but they are arrogant, petty, egotistical, and selfish.

We still think that they are very knowledgeable and they are wonderful. However, their being is all messed up and they create more problems in the world than they solve, even through what they create. However, knowledge must become combined with being. That is what made Moses such an incredible man. Moses invented too. Moses was a scientist, a religious leader, and a political leader. He knew geography.

Moses knew where the nations were because that was part of the Egyptian power empire. The Egyptian pharaohs knew 70 languages. God was not making a stupid mistake when He put Moses in the house of a pharaoh. Moses understood astronomy, geography and medicine. He knew how to transmute matter and how to process gold and silver. He understood how to do amazing things. He knew how it all worked.

There are people who are called to purely do spiritual activity because doing so helps the manifestation of the heavenly into the physical realm. However, knowledge must be accompanied by some comparable progress in being. So engage the Seven Spirits of God. The way you engage is you continue to be intimate with God. You do the ordinary activities because the Seven Spirits will engage you in practical, everyday happenings.

Engaging them in heaven is not going to do you any good because they need to come down and help you manifest in this realm. You can enjoy them in heaven. I see the lady Wisdom all the time.

There is a way I get the revelation I am giving you. The way I do it is by reading something I have never read before. I do not have to understand it. By the time I finish, the lady Wisdom shows up. When I begin to teach, it's as if I've studied this material for 20 years. Sometimes I have studied it just one hour. Nevertheless, she engages me and causes me to till the field, to till the garden that God has put me in my daily walk.

To engage the Spirit of the Fear of the Lord is to constantly self-examine before the Lord. Until human beings come to realize their complete insignificance they cannot grasp the vastness of God. However, until they also realize their complete significance, they cannot grasp the vastness of God.

It is a proportionate perspective of yourself that causes the Spirit of the Fear of the Lord to engage you. It is not fear as such, it is awe.

It is a sense of awe at the nature of God. How do you engage it? You engage by looking at the nature of God and looking at your nature. When you come to the point where you realize that God, who is infinite, contracted Himself to live in you, and that simple contraction is bigger than the universe, you will engage like that all the time. You will breathe it in. When you do that, it changes your perspective. You engage, then all of a sudden, the awe of the holiness of God is overtaking you. I am not talking about theory. I am talking about daily things that I do to engage.

How do I engage the Spirit of Counsel? What does the word counsel mean? In the Hebrew tradition counsel does not just mean instruction, it also means encouragement. To develop the Spirit of Counsel, you need to speak certain things to yourself. There are some things I've written about myself that I speak out to counsel and encourage myself in the Lord.

When it says David encouraged himself in the Lord, that's the Spirit of Counsel. You engage by speaking back to your soul. You examine your soul, you ask yourself questions, the hard questions. You make sure that you answer honestly. In counsel, you also engage the Spirit of Encouragement. You do not take condemnation into yourself.

The Seven Spirits of God are not the Holy Spirit. They are individual personalities created by God. Their role in the lives of humans is to tutor us into being fully mature sons. They work by relationship. To engage them is to start a relationship, based in honor. The Seven Spirits have always been interested in you. Your part is to consciously respond with intentionality.

THE KINGSHIP TRIAD: JUDAH, ZEBULUN & ISSACHAR

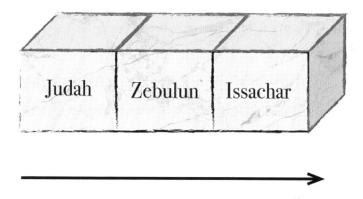

Let us look at the next 3 nested heavens of the 12 and their natures as they are revealed in the blessing of Jacob (Gen 49). As we understand the natures connected to each of these heavens we will be able to process them in or lives. This will free us from the fallen nature of each son / heaven in us and release us into our true nature. You are making the transition from Priesthood to Kinship. You are taking that big leap from your animalistic self into being a human! Yes, these 3 heavens deal with our Kingship. This is so you can judge and handle wealth, like your Father in heaven.

THE KINGSHIP TRIAD

Son:	Son:	Son:
Judah	**Zebulun**	**Issachar**
Meaning:	Meaning:	Meaning:
Rulership	**Exalted/Enthroned**	**Heard**
Dimension:	Dimension:	Dimension:
Kingship	**Adventurer**	**Time & Eternity**
Persona:	Persona:	Persona:
Mercy	**Power**	**Beauty**

⟶

The reason God wants to give you wealth is to train you to get to the point where you are able to release it out of your hand, so you are independent of it. You are certain and speak your sovereignty over the material world. However, how do you know how to have sovereignty over something that you have never experienced? So get that belief that poverty is a blessing out of your head.

This is why many of us who are poor are irresponsible. We work hard. That is not the point. When we get wealth, we are consumed by it. When wealth comes, it's God's way of trying to train you to assert your sovereignty over the material world. So get as much wealth as you can get. The key question is "Are you sovereign over it?" Do you go with everybody's emotions? Are you

> **"** The reason God wants to give you wealth is to train you to get to the point where you are able to release it out of your hand, so you are independent of it. **"**

controlled by everybody you meet? Do you get agitated by everybody's nonsensical behavior? You are conformed to them.

The Bible did not say, "do not relate to the world." It said, "be not conformed to the world." That is, you shouldn't be in such a state that you need people so much that every whim of their nonsensical behavior affects you at a deep level. You can't sleep because some person said something to you yesterday, or because you said some stupid things yourself. You are attached to these things. You allow yourself to be intrinsically connected to them which doesn't allow you then to minister to God, because you're not a sovereign.

When you go beyond the point of experience in Levi, you are going to be tested in all of these realms. And you want to be. You want to train yourself to get wealth. Then when you get wealth be sovereign over it. Think of the guys who gain wealth and all of a sudden in the middle of their lives just decide to give the wealth away. That person has mastered the material world. Those who don't have any wealth say, "gimme, gimme..." And they lose. You are counting your change on your bed. You lose 25 cents and you cry all day. You have not really learned how to handle material wealth.

However, God wants you to deal with it. That is why I think that the people who preach wealth are preaching it the wrong way. They do not understand it is training. You have to get to the point where you see it, you own it, you have it, but you hold it with an open hand. You do not commit yourself to people (I am not saying don't make a commitment in terms of marriage. Just don't throw yourself into people).

You just have to take them with a grain of salt. She's a kid and she's right. You love them, but you have to guard your heart with all diligence because guess what? People will reach in to your life and, whatever it is they can do to make it hurt, they will do.

You do it to people too. Part of it is that we are all being trained on how to act sovereignly. We are to love people but not allow our capacity to minister to God to be diminished by human tendencies. Now that is what Jesus meant when He says to follow him you must deny yourself and leave/despite your family - your father, mother, brother, sister, wife - all the intrinsic emotional connections. He says you have to deny them - that is, you have to step out of it. You still love them.

> **"** But do you know why God also wants you to have wealth? It is because when you have wealth, your wealth is a strong wall of defense. **"**

When you get to this point, if you get to the point where you begin to develop because now you are beginning to think rationally, then there is a stepping out into sovereignty. You have empathy, but you are not attached. The things people say don't really matter to you anymore.

But do you know why God also wants you to have wealth? It is because when you have wealth, your wealth is a strong wall of defense. What people say does not matter. When you are poor, everything somebody says matters. That is God's way of training you not to make things matter so much. So stop thinking you need to be poor in order to be holy and righteous because that is just silly.

Some young people that are in ministry say, "I'm just living my life from day to day." They are one of the people who get attached to the material in such a way. Even though you think you are independent of it, you are not. You have never been tested. So look for opportunities for God to bless you so that you can have enough to train your spiritual independence. Because God will do it. He wants to give you the kingdom. So when are you going to have time to practice?

This doesn't mean if you are poor that you are a terrible person. I am just saying if we are poor, those of us who are poor, we have not been trained on how to be independent of the material. That is why poor people buy the most expensive items and the most insignificant items. They'll buy a tennis shoe for $350 and then, at the end of the month, they don't have enough money because they have no control over the material.

Let us consider one of the richest men in the world who is worth over $US 60 billion and has lived in the same house for 30 years! He feels no compulsion to go compete with anybody. However, guys without money are the ones who bought $10 million dollar houses. They were not able to pay for them and their houses were taken. It is not because they lost their job, it is just because they could not pay for it. The training is important.

Let us get back to the heavenly dimensions. When you get to certain places, the way God trains you is to train you to get wealth. You will be tempted. Power will be offered to you in this level. Things will be shown to you that will make you think everybody else is stupid because it is a training. How much power can you handle?

After you have done the first 3 levels you will get to Judah. With Judah, there is a leap that will cause you to encounter Ariel Yehudah, who is the king. Let's assume that you are training yourself in sovereignty. This is where you are now sovereign. You begin to deal directly with the Father and with heaven. It is the first place where you actually see a throne that is not a throne of judgment, but a throne of relationship.

In the other levels, you are judging. You have to. Always remember that judgment is not over something out there. The judgment is always about what is happening inside of you. However, here you are in this second triad, a place of relationship with the Father. Yavodah. Yod, Vav, Dalet, Heh. If we calculate it, it is 25. 2 + 5 is 7. This is the kingly sacrifice which operates in rest. It is the heaven in which the King first makes His appearance. It is the beginning of the Sabbath. Now you have entered into rest.

> **"** When you get to that place where you actually have stripped away all the material, you are still worship. Sovereignty in relating to the King happens here. You are relating to God as King. **"**

Remember, throughout all the other levels you are having this agitation because things have to be stripped. Now you have come to Levi (or come to Judah) and your priesthood is now affirmed. It is in this place, when you come into this heavenly dimension, that you find yourself worshiping.

When you get to that place where you actually have stripped away all the material, you are still worship. Sovereignty in relating to the King happens here. You are relating to God as King.

JUDAH: THE DIMENSION OF KINGSHIP AND MERCY

Judah, thou art he whom thy brethren shall praise: thy hand shall be in the neck of thine enemies; thy father's children shall bow down before thee. Judah is a lion's whelp: from the prey, my son, thou art gone up: he stooped down, he crouched as a lion, and as an old lion; who shall rouse him up? The sceptre shall not depart from Judah, nor a lawgiver from between his feet, until Shiloh come; and unto him shall the gathering of the people be. Binding his foal unto the vine, and his ass's colt unto the choice vine; he washed his garments in wine, and his clothes in the blood of grapes. His eyes shall be red with wine, and his teeth white with milk. (Gen 49:8-12)

The first dimension of the second triad is that of Judah. This is where you become a judge. There are not only thrones of kingship in Judah but of judgment, because when kingship comes you must also stand as a judge. You are looking at things. You are questioning things - because only a person with an independent will can be a king.

> **"** Only a person with a clear identity can be a king or a queen and rule in their region. **"**

Only a person with a clear identity can be a king or a queen and rule in their region. Once you get into this dimension, God begins to show you hidden truths and starts teaching you how to form things and terraform domains. Remember, God created you in His image. What God is trying to do is to get you into His image so that, when you create something, it reflects both you and Him. There is a lion here which roars into the ground to control the atmosphere and to transform it.

Something has happened - what we call *transmutation*. It is a spiritual evolution that happens in which there is a leap. Remember I told you it is the formation of the cherubic. Now the will is formed, but there is a cherubic principle being formed here. What does a cherubim do? A cherubim has eight wings, eight arms, four faces and two legs.

What do his legs look like? Bronze, gold, diamond, platinum or titanium? That of a normal man? No, a cherub looks like he has the feet of a cow/ox! The leg has a hoof. It is like that of a calf that is all the way down to the hoof. It has hooves. If you saw a cherubim it would look exactly like a painting of Satan, who has hooves? That is right, it would look exactly like that. It is a problem if you keep thinking that these creatures that are fallen are so different from the ones that are in heaven.

The only difference is that these fallen ones cannot do without a material being. However, the holy ones are spirit, so they can abide as spirit and function as spirit. The fallen ones need matter to be constant. They have a constant attachment to matter and, they are constantly on the lookout for human beings to make them unclean. That is why an idol worship and its place is always dirty. Everywhere that people worship idols it is dirty, unclean and stinks. Even in the best of temples they have to clean it every day.

Now, as we look at the cherubim, let us calculate: 8 wings + 8 arms = 16. 16 + 4 faces = 20. 20 + 2 legs = 22. In basic numbers system 2 + 2 = 4. One can see, given that the name of God has 4 letters, that cherubim may be seen as carrying the majesty of the Name. Looking at the Cherub in Ezekiel we could learn some things that will help us see what God is doing in the life of the believer who enters into this realm carries with them the Name and operates in the name.

> Each of them had four faces and four sets of wings.
> ₇ Their legs were straight and their feet were like a calf's hoof, and they gleamed like burnished bronze ₈ Under their wings on their four sides were human (four pairs of hands). As for the faces and wings of the four of them. (Eze 1:6-8 NAS)

Now if we count the other person that is riding the cherub, that is 23. There is somebody on the throne inside the cherub.

Scripture says 4 sets of wings. It says with 2 he flew. 2 covered the legs. 2 covered his face. So at least there are two wings for each face making them eight wings. You take the cherubim the way they appear, you find out it actually ends up having eight wings. Therefore, you consider all of the descriptions in Scripture, not just 1 vision.

There are 4 wheels. One may be led to argue that they are two, but I believe the wheels are 4 because it says the wheels within the wheels. Now you have this cherubim that has, if you look at everything in it, 22 + 4. Four wheels. That is a chariot. Therefore, it is a wheel within a wheel. In addition, it went in every direction without turning. I use the 4 to represent both the inherence of the Name and the nature of The Lord God who is everywhere at once and, as such, nonlocal in his movement. That means it can go east without turning, it can go west without turning, north and south without turning and do so merely by the spirit or thought. Wherever the spirit desires, *there they are.*

You have to look at how it appears. When we then add the wheel within the wheels we have 22 + 4 = 26. Again in basic numerical gematria of this 26 will equal 8 - which will represent new creation or the capacity to cause constant renewal based on the fact that the name of the Lord is within and without. Plus the person sitting on the throne because it is not the face of the cherubim that is sitting on the throne. It is not the human face of the cherubim sitting on the throne. It is One like the Son of Man. Remember that we are talking about the cherubic formation. There will be more explanation or application of this numbering process in my upcoming book on the Hebrew alphabet.

When you begin to become sovereign, then your covering cherub begins to form. Moreover, there are different kinds of cherubim. That is why Ezekiel saw different kinds of them. That is why John saw different kinds of them. If you read carefully, sometimes Ezekiel says, "The same one that I saw." Sometimes he does not say, "The same one that I saw."

Become a rational human being. Rational does not mean that you need proof for everything. The Western world thinks that if you are rational, it means you need to have concrete material proof for everything. There are objective proofs and there are subjective proofs. Nevertheless, it does not need to be materialistic.

When you get to the point where God touches your intellect and opens it up, He releases a dimension, which is the 4th dimension. It is considered the 4th heaven of kingship, which is the dimension of creation - not the dimension of judgment. The dimension of judgment is the dimension of the fallen nature of man. The dimension of kingship is the dimension of creation.

The priesthood deals with the fallen nature of man (first triad). The kingship(second triad) deals with the capacity of a human being to create from the fourth dimension because it completes the cycle of the name of God.

Judah is the dimension of kingship. However, even the dimension of kingship still has vestiges of things you must deal with in order to come to fullness. It is easier now, because there is a greater freedom. Many of you who go into the heavens operate in this dimension. Once God has dealt with you (or even when God has not) He begins to show you revelation Himself.

YOU MUST DEAL WITH PRIESTHOOD ISSUES

Sometimes He does not take you through all the 3 dimensions in the first triad. He just takes you directly here to Judah. But here's the problem when you get there. You experience kingship without the independent will. You experience all the beauty, you experience God talking to you and you see things being created. However, you have not developed the will to create yourself. That will can only be developed after you have gone through the first 3 dimensions and the fire (menorah).

God sends you back to the first triad dimensions after you have all the other experiences in the Judah dimension. So you're having this great experience of God showing you the heavenlies, the kingship, Him sitting upon the throne, putting you upon the throne and you're rejoicing - then after a while you're going to realize you have no will of your own to be able to create. God's going to say, "No, you need to go back down and develop your will so that you can be a king." You have to go back down and deal with priesthood issues.

Some of us are so carried away with all those heavenly, kingly experiences that we never develop. We never really deal with the previous dimensions. We do not deal with the cow/ox. We do not deal with the lower lion. We do not deal with the eagle looking for flesh. God loves you and He will always send you to deal with those because they are important for your kingship.

Part of David's problem was that one aspect of his life was never dealt with - Reuben. David's sexuality is tied to his violence. The focus of God is to deal with all the symptoms of your life so that your sexual center can be dealt with. If your sexual center is not dealt with you're going to make a mess of yourself. It is going to affect everything you try to create, including your business and other areas of your life.

The reason you deal with the first 3 dimensions is the sexual center. Remember the circumcision process that the Jews do is to focus on that sexual center because that is where most of your energy is. Many of the other energies you use are wasted. It is a symbolic center of your creativity. In kingship, you now have to deal with your sovereign self. Your "I". You have to deal with that productive center. That is where David was caught. It is the same place Judah was caught. However, it is not sexuality in terms of incest. It is sexuality in terms of controlling those around you and using other people.

What was Judah's problem? He is a king wearing his bangles and walking with his staff, and he sees a prostitute on the side of the road. There is a lot of symbolism in this story. He gets his own daughter-in-law pregnant without knowing because he's blinded by his desire and blinded by his power. Blinded by his gifting.

It was the same with David. God does not take away kingship from David because of it but He deals with him. However, it costs David because he could not build the temple. When God says in Chronicles 28, "you're a man of blood," He is not referring only to all the wars that David had fought (Though In Chronicles 28:3 God directly mentions war. "But God said unto me, Thou shalt not build a house for my name, because thou hast been a man of war, and hast shed blood." This "thou has shed blood" is very interesting because warfare blood is not considered a hindrance for divine service. So I think this verse should be read in conjunction with punishment for shedding of the blood if Uriah) "*Now therefore, the sword shall never depart from your house, because you have despised Me and have taken the wife of Uriah the Hittite to be your wife.*" (2 Sa 12:10 NAS)

David may have been able to build the temple if he did not kill Uriah and took his wife. That unnecessary bloodshed is the issue here. That is what God is talking about. God is speaking directly to the death of Uriah, which was the result of sexuality. What I am telling you is not terrible. Please do not think I am one of these prudes and these preachers who focus on this area. I am telling you how to work with your own body. You need to work with your own body and understand that these things are highly significant for your own growth.

This is where what I call the 'third spiritual body' begins to develop (See teaching on Navigating the Tabernacle at www.aactev8.com). It is when you learn to be sovereign and you do not act unless you have thought about it and your will is committed to it. It is better to argue with God, and even say no, than to just be a slave. God does not want slaves. God only wants slaves who have been free, who then freely committed themselves to slavery. Do you get the difference? Therefore, everything that you do with God must come out of a will where you say, "I choose to obey." If you must obey, you are not free - and this is how most Christians operate. So go through the process so you can choose to obey.

The issues that I used to struggle with, when I started questioning them in my life, started just going away. When I started really facing them and saying, "Okay, I need to understand how this works. Come on. Anger, come, come, come, come. I want to feel how it feels." When I started really trying to experience how it actually felt, it felt so yucky that my own body began to be repulsed by it. Conversely, the more I self-justified, the more this poison tasted sweet.

THE REAL YOU

So we move to the kingship level dimension of heaven. The kingship level for man begins the next dimension of experience in heaven. Now you are going to experience different kinds of issues. Your true issue is power and sexuality, which hang around trying to get you to think, "Man, I can kill Uriah and take his wife."

Fourth dimensional heaven is where you take that big leap from your animalistic self into being a human, and you begin to develop the third level body. This is where you come in touch with your physical body. Then you come in touch with the second body, which some people call 'aura'. Now you are coming in touch with a cherubic body. However, in this level, you must learn to engage the four faces (see "Meditation on the four faces of God and the four letter name", "Navigating the tabernacles" at www.aactev8.com. Plus check our YouTube channel).

You must engage the four faces. You must engage them constantly in order to keep them in balance. Then your will, as the son of man, sits in the driver's seat as the master. It submits to God freely. Only a king has a right to submit to a king. Only a king can give a territory to another king and enter into covenant. At that point, you are able to enter into covenant and the devil gets scared of you.

In all these things you were doing before this the devil was not scared of you because it is not you. You have not really stood as the sovereign that God created to make a lot of choices. You will hear people say, "It is just his schooling speaking. It is just his friends speaking. Oh, it is just Joe that he met 20 years ago is now talking through him. She is just speaking from Maria or Patricia that she knew when she was growing up." People are not their real selves. You may think it is your real self but it is not.

People are the result of the 'selves' that are hanging around. But when that sovereign person shows up, something amazing happens. That is why the devil, the world and nature fight so hard to keep that sovereign person hidden. Even religion fights to keep that sovereign person hidden. The things you call spirituality are designed to obfuscate that person. It was in the fall that this true person was hidden and pushed down.

Part of redemption is to bring that sovereign person out. Therefore, when you bring the "I," the real "I" out, we can say with Paul "it is no longer I who live" (Gal 2:20 NAS). But it is not the "I" that is the true him that no longer lives. He goes on to say, "The life that *I* live now..." - there are about three "I"s now - "and the life which I now live in the flesh I live by faith in the Son of God, who loved me". So this true "I" can submit to the Son of God and live by the grace of the Son of God because it is free. Do you know before Jesus accepts you, He makes you free? That is what He does? "If the Son therefore shall make you free, ye shall be free indeed" (John 8:36). He makes you free. Do you know that when He makes you free you now have a choice to reject Him?

If somebody wants you to serve them do they set you free? No. God walks in a different way. The first thing God does is set you free. That is why He set Adam in the garden free. This is how Adam could choose. Adam chose to relate to somebody that he could be enslaved with rather than choosing to be a free person.

You need to be free to be a king. Free to choose. The real you and not your upbringing or earthly influences. Only then you are truly choosing.

Now, if you are a sovereign "I", your action is more impactful than if you are not. Most of the activity that we do has no impact. We cannot even change little things. However, as a sovereign, your action is taken seriously by the whole universe. That is why it is harder on us.

It does not mean we don't get forgiven but things we do create a lot more ripples. Now we can be cleansed because of the blood of Jesus Christ. This is the reconstitution of everything that has been messed up. But why mess up so you can reconstitute it? Therefore, you have to start working on your Reuben, Simeon and Levi materialistic and people issues. It is preparation for the Judah, Issachar, and Zebulun.

PRAISE OF MAN

Jacob says of Judah "You are him whom your brother shall praise." Remember, there are sounds in the other three levels we dealt with. However, they are not really sounds of praise. They are cacophonous sounds and it's difficult to make them out. But in this dimension, the sound begins to become distinct. It becomes a sound of praise. But here's the thing - the first sound of praise is not praise being given to God!

It is praise that his own brethren, those he has relationship with, begin to give him. Here is also the test of hubris because people say all kinds of nice things about you. Jesus said to be careful when men say wonderful things about you! (Luke 6:26). Now your emotions have been refined. The more your emotions get refined the more you want something because your nature is like God's nature.

You want praise because God receives praise. So now, you have this thing in you that is like God, but it wants to take whatever belongs to God and point it to itself. Your brethren will praise you but that is not the issue. There is no sin in your brethren praising you. But the first sound you are going to hear is the sound of your own hype, like "I'm good". Then you begin to spiritually brag.

You say, "Oh, no, it's the Lord's doing. But hey, I want to testify." Therefore, you start testifying and soon you are 'testi-lying'. Come on, there's so much testi-lying in the church. "I was somewhere and the Lord moved. There were clouds and fire. I saw a 50,000 foot angel."

However, your brethren will talk well about you. All of a sudden there is a radiance coming out of you because you have now stepped into that sovereignty. There is this brilliance flowing from you. Without you even saying stories, people are coming to you. All of a sudden, your head becomes bigger than the house in which you live.

Your creativity goes off the roof. The greatest example of this is Absalom - "I'm a prince, I'm handsome, I can ride, I've got long hair, and everybody's talking about how much more handsome I am than my father." If you are a young preacher, you begin to think you're so smart. You're smarter than your dumb pastor who didn't go to seminary. You bring a curse on yourself. Therefore, you think it does not really matter what you do because you are really gifted.

OPERATING AS A KING

Let's keep reading. "Your hand shall be on the neck of your enemies." This is the place of victory. When you operate in this heaven Satan will not go there. Demons do not go there because when they show up, they are decimated. It's a place of victory. This is a place of the sword carriers as in Psalm 149:6-9;

> **"** You have to develop the four faces that sit on that throne - Lion, Ox, Eagle, Man - reflecting the glory of the Father. **"**

"Let the high praises of God be in their mouth, And a two-edged sword in their hand, To execute vengeance on the nations, And punishments on the peoples; To bind their kings with chains, And their nobles with fetters of iron; To execute on them the written judgment - This honor have all His saints"

However, this is about executing vengeance, not judgment. They are two different things. When you are here in Judah, you operate with royal authority. Your father's children shall bow before you. Very few people who actually make it to this realm understand their own calling as kings. Many people will make it to this level but still have too much of Reuben, too much of Simeon and too much of the material. When they get into this realm they cannot really operate as a king. They still operate as a subject.

You don't want to be like that. It is a training that happens. When you're sovereign, "your brethren shall bow." I want to say this now with all due humility. When you get to this point where you are operating as a king, there are many other beings in that realm who come and fall at your feet - but again, you don't let it go to your head.

The throne of kingship here is not the throne of God, but it is your throne. This is a throne that you sit on. This is where you are cherubic, because your cherubic nature has been formed, and your cherubic angel is now formed. Your throne is set. "Your throne, O Lord, is forever." God builds a throne. He builds it. Your throne is built in this Judah place. Because this is the place from which the Messianic principle emerges.

It is the first place where you, as a man, reign. Now you're reigning over yourself and you're also reigning over others. Your throne is there and you have the cherubim that now cover your throne because you're beginning to be like your Father. Everybody who operates in this level has the cherubic covering. Even they themselves can become a cherubic.

You have to develop the four faces that sit on that throne - Lion, Ox, Eagle, Man - reflecting the glory of the Father. Now you roar. You roar over an area. This is where your mountain is formed. The dragons you have to deal with in this region are the facets of pride and worship because these issues will arise and you will experience them.

You open your mouth and angels are there. You move and there they are. However, you have to keep your heart, because out of it are the issues of life. You have to make sure what comes out of your heart does not repel the angels and does not cause a falling back.

All of a sudden, you are seeing the Lord Jesus. You are seeing Him almost everywhere you turn. Why? Because He is training you to be a king and He is the King of Kings, which makes him the king over kings! He is not the King of paupers, He is the King of Kings - and you are one of the kings that are under Him. So now you have come and your throne is being trained because He is king over you as king. He's the King of Kings, of everybody.

So here your kingship begins to manifest. This dimension of heaven is so important. Moreover, the Bible says if we suffer with Him then we shall reign with Him (2 Tim 2:12). Remember that. You go through all this process so you can reign. You don't reign because you are a child of God. You reign because you are a trained king.

"Judah is a lion's whelp." This is where your lion nature is formed. You learn you are not the big lion. You are a lion's whelp. You are a lion in training. You are crouching under the Great Lion as a little lion. You are learning to be a son. So you stoop down, you bow, you crouch. You act like an old lion because you are imitating the old lion. And He begins to breathe over you. He begins to roar over you, and you begin to roar back. He roars over you, and you then roar back.

When roaring, there's an echo of formative sound happening in you. While you are a lion in experience, you are an older lion by interaction. The nature of the older lion is being formed in you. Anyone who rouses you up, any demon, any power that rouses you up, is decimated. There is no time for going to court. This is head chopping time. That is what I mean when I mentioned that you do not constantly go to the court of Heaven for a judgment. A king does not go to court. He goes and takes vengeance.

Everything that tries to cross your mountain is dealt with. It is a dangerous thing when you first get up there. This is what Elijah had to learn when he first got on his mountain. He did not realize what power he had. Consider what Jesus says about the servant who begins to mistreat his brothers and sisters because the master is gone.

"The scepter shall not depart from Judah, nor a lawgiver from between his feet." It did not say that the scepter shall not depart from God. This is a principle of rulership. This is where you get your scepter. You are given a scepter. A scepter is the stick by which you walk, but also the stick by which you give permission for anything to come in and go out. You stretch out your scepter, and whatever being comes in is accepted. You don't stretch it out, and they stay where they are.

If they cross the line, they are killed or are dealt with. "A lawgiver from between his feet." It is between your feet. I keep coming back to the issue of sexuality because that's where the Messiah is hidden. If you read the Book of Revelation, it says these are "they who knew no women" (Rev 14:4), who follow the Messiah wherever He goes. It is an issue of the protection of your energy, your sexual energy, which comes directly from God. It serves as the center of your creativity, and the place of your transmutation of the energy of God into material manifestation. It sits in between your legs.

So control your energy. Just because you are not committing fornication does not mean you're not wasting your sexual energy. You're wasting it in all that agitation - the anger and the unnecessary activity you do that uses up your emotions so that your energy is not directed towards your creativity. This means you're not bringing forth the new.

"Until Shiloh comes and unto Him shall the gathering of the people be." Shiloh means tranquility - that which belongs to, that to whom it belongs, which is the resting place. Until you come to the place of rest, nothing belongs to you. The law of the Sabbath is also the foundational principle of kingship.

KINGS MANAGE WEALTH

In this dimension, as we deal with it, we begin to see some other things. "Binding his foal unto the vine." The foal is a donkey, a beast of burden. It is not a cow as a cow does not carry treasures.

The ancients carried their treasures on donkeys. A man could be riding his horse and he will have a donkey on the side. It carries treasure and it can carry more than a cow can carry, small as it is. It can go for hours and hours of travel and not faint, even when a horse will faint. In addition, a donkey will not follow just anybody. It is the most stubborn thing. I have seen a donkey lay down and ten men try to get it up. It will not budge. It is also attached to its master.

It is a treasure carrier but it's tied to a vine. What is a vine? A vine always symbolizes fruitfulness. Here in this dimension, God begins to teach you how to prosper, how to become fruitful, how to carry treasure, how to preserve what He gives you for the kingdom.

"Unto the choice vine. He washed his garment in wine, and his clothes in the blood of grapes." It is the same thing. There are certain things about kingship. A sour and unhappy king is a dangerous person because he chops heads off everywhere. We know that from King Henry VIII. He throws a temper tantrum and somebody's head rolls. It is not good for a king to be easily angered. That is why you have to deal with the first 3 dimensions. There is an overflow of joy in the presence of a good king. This is what God is teaching you.

Before Jesus left, He said, "My peace I give unto you...that you may be joyful. That you may have joy and that your joy may be full. Be joyful. I have overcome the world. (John 14 - 16)" There is an overflow. The wine represents the overflowing joy.

God wants to do several things. He wants to teach you how to handle wealth, how to make wealth and how to transmute into actual wealth. This level is where you begin to ask to take things from the heavens and manifest them on earth. You tie them to your vine. That is a Jack and the Beanstalk concept - it is all in the story.

You go up there and you come down the vine with the golden treasure. You tie the donkey, which is now a tribe burden bearer, which carries the treasure to and from the vine. The vine becomes a pathway between heaven and earth, between the spiritual realm and the physical realm, where you take things that are there and bring them here.

These pathways are paved with joy and rest. Rest in the body, rest in the emotion, rest in all the motions. "He that believes, (shall not agitate or) shall not make haste," says Isaiah 28:16. This is very vital as you move in this dimension. "My peace I give unto you" says the Lord, "not as the world gives (John 14:27)." He's called Sar shalom. He replaces the garments of mourning with the garments of praise and joy.

They are the two pathways for manifesting from there to here.

That is what worship is supposed to do. In spite of everything, David was a very happy man. With the exception of a few psalms - when he was suffering under Saul, and when he was crying after he killed Uriah - most of his psalms were "O Lord I will do this..." He understood that a mind at rest and filled with joy has access to divine creativity. One joyful and peaceful person can change the atmosphere of a whole nation.

This is why Mozart is still the best musician. It is because he wrote as a kid who was so joyful about everything. The music just makes you skip. There is something about it. Anyway, the praise of the brethren is now taken in, solidified in the "I," and as the "I" sovereignly submits to God, the praise that is given to the "I" is also sovereignly given back to God.

WE MUST BE THOROUGH WITH OURSELVES

This would be a good place to reinforce making sure you fully develop your cherubic nature.

Babies want their way and they want it now. What is happening is that once you begin to deal with your desires, you allow the angels to bring the water. Remember, the water is also the basis for the growth of a lot of areas. If you do not deal with the water of Reuben, you cannot really grow.

When you actually overcome this, when you actually deal with this, your first angelic nature appears. It is really a watery nature. It is like coming out of a womb. It is the dew. It becomes crystallized dew. In Hebrew, it is called 'afribri' the angel of the dew. It is in you. It is not outside of you. When you begin to overcome, then your soul takes on its first body - resurrection body. People that deal with the other areas will start talking about your "aura." But I do not like the word aura because it doesn't deal with the actual principle of the body.

> " God wants to do several things. He wants to teach you how to handle wealth, how to make wealth and how to transmute into actual wealth. "

If you look at 1 Corinthians 15, it says there are fleshly bodies of all kinds. When you deal with the issue of flesh, you have to deal with the different kinds of flesh you have - because you kill them. Now you kill this, you kill that. You need to deal with your animal flesh, your bird flesh, your reptilian flesh. These are in descending order of carnality and demonization which occurs in people who refuse to enter the kingdom through Christ or who practice descent and ascension through darkness and not light. All these flesh are being dealt with here through the person and sacrifice of Jesus Christ. This is what the blood of Jesus Christ does. This is where you keep applying the blood. You keep going to the cross of Jesus Christ. You keep allowing the blood of Jesus Christ to cleanse and deal with your flesh. This is where you have communion.

You do not let it go. You do it every day. You keep taking communion. You participate in it. You implore the blood. You operate under the blood of Jesus Christ. This is where your DNA is getting transformed because the water is where you can move into anything you want to do, until you get transmuted.

When you have dealt with the Simeon dimension, it doesn't mean that a lot of the other issues don't try to come back in. The sexual issue still tries to creep in. The lies still try to creep in. You know the issues, but now your body has been so separated from the fleshly levels so that it is actually doing what it was meant to do.

That is, it is actually feeling. It is not feeling as a reaction. It is feeling because you are conscious

> **"** There are no shortcuts to being a king like Jesus, the King of Kings. **"**

of it. So your first angelic manifestation is the actual angel of your physical body because your body was created by God to do certain things right and to intuit certain things emotionally right.

There are no short cuts to being a king like Jesus, the King of Kings.

ZEBULUN: THE DIMENSION OF THE ADVENTURER AND POWER

"Zebulun shall dwell at the haven of the sea; and he shall be for an haven of ships; and his border shall be unto Zidon." (Gen 49:13)

Zebulun is the 6th son of Jacob. His name means "exalted". It works this way. There is the dimension of Judah that is of kingship. The building on the throne. The next one is 'exaltation'. What is exaltation? The text says, "Zebulun shall dwell..." It literally means enthronement, to be enthroned. So here is the king, the throne is built, and Zebulun is exalted.

RULING THE SEAS

Zebulun dwells by the sea. How does the throne of God appear in the Book of Revelation? The throne is way above and the Sea of Glass is below it. So in order to get to the throne of God you must go through the Sea of Glass. However, in this, Judah's throne is established and the sea is in front, not way below. Ships come and dock at that place. Look at the image in your head. "Dwells in the haven of the sea and he shall be for haven of ship, and his border shall be unto Sidon." What do you know about Sidon? The city of Sidon was one of the richest cities in the world until it was captured by Alexander the Great.

Alexander captured Sidon, he destroyed Tyre in 332 BC.

Who do you know in the Bible that came from Sidon (Zidon)? Where was Jezebel from? She was the daughter of Ethbaal, King of Sidon (I Kings 16:31). Doesn't the Bible always speak of Tyre and Sidon? So why be exalted upon the sea that borders one of the most wicked cities? Let me explain. Satan had his throne across the water. Therefore, they had to retire in that place. That is where the King of Tyre was paired to. Sidon and Tyre were connected. They were like twins, connected on the other side. Now consider Zebulun and Judah. Judah is exalted by the sea and his ship comes and docks at Zebulun, where Judah has been exalted but on the other side.

> **Operating in this level means you go in as a king and you literally sit there in the heavens, in your authority.**

Operating in this level means you go in as a king and you literally sit there in the heavens, in your authority. There are people who do this. People who experience this sovereignty, by this sea, and have the power to go to the other side and literally set people free. So ships come and they literally are able to go to the other side, release what has been taken and kept captive, put it on ships and bring it back to the shore. That is what the king does.

This is not the Sea of Glass. This is the sea upon which the kingship is given to those who have developed sovereignty, who operate in order to bring people from one side to the other. A king who can bring the riches that are held on one side to the other and release the things that are held and were captured. These are things that have been swallowed and are released; they are put on ships - which literally means transportation devices.

It is like taking your donkey and tying it to a vine and putting everything on it and bringing it from that dimension to this dimension. With Zebulun, now you have the same thing, but you need to have the ship that carries the treasure from that place. In the previous realm of Judah, this is the manifestation of the flow from the throne of God that is carried on your donkey. In Zebulun you do it by ship because there's a divide.

That is what Jesus did. People ask me, "Why does the Bible say that there's a division between Abraham and Lot?" (Gen 13). Only kings who have been created sovereignly, and who have dealt with their issues, can cross, conquer, and take the captives from that side to this side. That is the example of what Jesus showed us.

The reason you are being made into kings is because you are being given a certain royal authority to go and set the captives free. You put them on the sea and cross over, and you bring them to a good place. They are not your captives. You release them as a king. You bring them over and you hand them over to the King of Kings. You are setting people free.

Most people do not understand Nimrod. Most teachings look at Nimrod as a very terrible person and a very wicked person. They miss the statement that Nimrod was a mighty hunter in the presence of the Lord (Gen 10:9). Nimrod was a king. Nimrod ruled over 8 cities that were gateways and traps, if you can receive it. God gave him the grace to build those cities that still survive until today.

Maybe some of them were gateways to travel to dimensions. He was a hunter of beings that were coming to invade humanity to try to take and change the DNA of humanity. That is why it says, "as Nimrod, the mighty hunter, in the presence of the Lord."

In Deuteronomy 33:18 it says, "And of Zebulun He said: Rejoice, Zebulun, in thy going out." It is just very short. There is no long explanation. "Rejoice, Zebulun, in thy going out." A king goes out on excursions. Part of Judah's kingship is that he has joy.

The kingly joy is what leads them. What happens is the king goes out on Zebulun, exalted on the sea, and comes back on that sea. But what is the sea? The sea is people. People from every tribe, every tongue. That is in Revelation. The Bible defines it that way.

When you are exalted as a king, when you get to these dimensions, your job now is to operate at a level where your major objective is to go into dark places and release people. This is not intercession. This is not O Lord, please deliver such and such. You are not interceding with God, you are facing down the enemy. Until you are a king you can't face down the enemy and you get into spiritual warfare at your own peril.

Remember, it is not the Sea of Glass. That is in a higher heaven. This is a lower heaven and it is a turbulent sea. You don't go in there to deliver anybody you want to. You need an assignment. You need official papers. You need direction to go and deliver the people. If you go without an assignment you could probably succeed because God is merciful but it is always better to have an assignment and do one assignment at a time.

What happens with many people when they get a taste of the kind of power that they have in this realm and think they can go and do everything, then they overstep their boundaries. Even though those people can move on these kingly dimensions there are boundaries they must obey. People get messed up in spiritual warfare. They become casualties. They become possessed. A lot of things happen to people because they cross the boundary. They get caught up in the sea of emotions of the people who want to be rescued / delivered.

It happens to people who are ministers because they want to show that they can minister to everybody. So they stand for five hours and pray for anybody who comes. Then things begin to happen to their body and to other areas of their lives. So watch yourself.

In the dimension of Zebulun you go to places and you release. When you were back in the Levi dimension there were material things that were a temptation to you. You worked at releasing your attachment to them. Now you are a king. You can now go and deliver people without getting possessed by spirits. Do you know what we call the things we own? Possessions. It is a demonic term. It is a possession, "He has so many possessions." Simply, he has been possessed by things.

Language is very important. We don't use the word possession just for things or objects. We use it for entities occupying other entities. If you possess something, it means your spirit is in it. You cannot possess something without being possessed by that thing. That is why God does all this dimensional work on you. So that you aren't captured by materiality.

The ancient Greeks, the Gnostics, followed a belief system we call Gnosticism. Like every human system, it is good in some ways and wrong in some ways. Where they talk about the spirit being caught in matter, they are right because we as human beings can get possessed by material things. Our light gets caught up in matter and cannot be released. We need other people to come and release us. It is much more difficult to be released from materialism than it is actually to be delivered from demonic possession.

There is a tendency to be intertwined with matter because you are part matter. So you do not know when it possesses you or when you possess it. However, when an entity from outside which is not matter possesses you, you can kick it out.

Remember, we had the gate from Levi, through the menorah, to Judah. I call it a quantum gate because there is a quantum shift that happens. So people that have been struggling with slavery all of a sudden become free and they can think for themselves. They do things from understanding. They understand purpose. They can stop forces and direct forces. They are now in the kingship dimensions. Their throne is built, their cherubic force is formed and their cherubic personality is out.

KINGLY ASSIGNMENTS

However, there is an assignment that comes. That assignment is to cross the sea into spiritual Sidon. It is physical but it's all symbolic. We go into Sidon and release people because that is where people are held captive. Remember, "The Spirit of the Lord *is* upon Me, Because He has anointed Me To preach the gospel to *the* poor; He has sent Me to heal *the* broken hearted, To proclaim liberty to *the* captives and recovery of sight to *the* blind, *To* set at liberty those who are oppressed" (Luke 4:18 NKJV). Therefore, you go and you set the captive free, but you do not stay there. You go, you do, and you come back. So you must therefore have a strategic sense.

Do not just do activity because you feel like doing it. If you operate in feelings as king you will die. When you operate in feelings, you get yourself involved in issues just because you feel sorry for someone. Someone is demon possessed or somebody has given himself over to Satan and you think you are the one to deliver them.

You may not be the one to deliver them. You get into that troubled sea and the person drags you down with him. In this kingly place you have to understand your specific assignment because now you are dealing with a particular kind of angelic ministration. Angelic ministration only comes one at a time. An angel has one assignment at a time, not two. If you try to do more things than what you are assigned by heaven you will get yourself in trouble.

I love the Zebulun activity because it is a going out, an effulgence, a shining forth over the sea. What stabilizes this sea? It is a sea that is bordering the Sea of Glass. You are facing the sea of men, of every tribe and tongue. Behind you is the Sea of Glass. Out of the throne that is behind you, which is the throne of the King of Kings, flow the four rivers that come into you from the garden in you. The garden in you is your heart. Out of that garden, rivers flow out of you that stabilize the sea of men, so you will be able to go into another place to rescue people and come back on your own stream, which flows from God.

What are these streams? Praise, Worship, Joy and Rest. The four rivers. These are the four garments that protect you when you go into that realm. The blood of Jesus is your protection but praise keeps you covered, your sound is worship, you experience joy, and you have rest which is faith.

What is the color of Judah? Green. Emerald. This signifies fertility, growth, production, fruitfulness and all the good things that come with it. What is the color of Zebulun? Sardonyx. Sardonyx is reddish. It is right in the text as the red of grapes. It is a different kind of emotion which is based on joy. You see, there is a redness that represents an emotional instability that rises - because there is a redness that comes with joy.

Then the next dimension on the list is Issachar. You see Judah, Zebulun, Issachar. Part of Zebulun's issues that you have to deal with is being a vagabond and wandering on the sea from one position to another, never landing in the heavens so that your kingship never comes to fruition. You do not stay in anything long enough for it to actually give birth.

It is not good to have a vagabond spirit. If you have an orphan spirit you are wandering from one person to another. Every one of these dimensions has its downside. Kingship has that Luciferian principle of trying to rise up against God and pride that brings you down. Remember, in every heaven, there is a possibility of hell.

ISSACHAR: THE DIMENSION OF TIME / ETERNITY AND BEAUTY

Issachar is a strong ass couching down between two burdens: $_{15}$ And he saw that rest was good, and the land that it was pleasant; and bowed his shoulder to bear, and became a servant unto tribute. (Gen 49:14-15)

I love Issachar. This is where you become the master of time. A king must understand times and seasons and be able to master them because his operation must come from his impact upon eternity. In Genesis 49:14, it says, "Issachar is a strong ass, crouching down between two burdens." Time and eternity. Night and day. Male and female. Outside and inside. Strong and lazy. Courage and cowardice.

"He saw that the rest was good." Remember the rest of the king? "He saw that the rest was good and the land that it was pleasant, and bowed his shoulder to bear, and became a servant unto tribute."

That is what Jacob saw in Issachar. Jacob saw strength and the capacity to carry. He saw the capacity to be a burden bearer but also that the experience of rest made Issachar lazy. The experience of pleasure made Issachar become a slave. Later we are going to look at some of the reasons why you have 1, 2, 3, 1, 2, 3. The triadic process helps balance out each other in such a way that they form gates for entrance into the next dimension, realms or sphere.

A KING BUILDS WEALTH

Deuteronomy 33:18. "...Issachar in your tents!" Rejoice in your tent. "They shall call the people unto the mountain. They shall offer sacrifices of righteousness; for they shall suck of the abundance of the sea and of the treasures hidden in the sand." Again, everything in this second triad deals with wealth, treasures and victory. God just made it that way. The first thing God does when Israel leaves Egypt is to give them wealth.

The first thing God does when He builds the Garden is put gold in the first river. "The gold of that land is good," (Gen 2:12). You cannot do this walk without wealth. The first thing that happened in Jesus' ministry was not the election of the Twelve. Do you know who provided for Jesus? The Magi brought gold and frankincense before the flight to Egypt. In His ministry, the ones who provided were "some women who had been healed of evil spirits and sicknesses: Mary who was called Magdalene, from whom seven demons had gone out, 3 and Joanna the wife of Chuza, Herod's steward, and Susanna, and many others who were contributing to their support out of their private means" (Luke 8:2-3 NAS) They provided for Him while He did ministry!

People want to talk about Jesus not having any money. He had kings' and

> " He had kings' and rulers' and governors' family members providing for Him. Read your Bible it's right there. You cannot play the philosopher or play the king without wealth. I think I am clearing up some misunderstanding for some people. "

rulers' and governors' family members providing for Him. Read your Bible it's right there. You cannot play the philosopher or play the king without wealth. I think I am clearing up some misunderstanding for some people.

We need to understand that if we have the idea that we can do kingdom ministry without money, we are lying to ourselves. You would be lying to yourself. You cannot do it without gold. The Master did not do it without gold but people always read the Scriptures the way they want to read the Scriptures. The apostles' first success was based on people who were wealthy, people who were willing to bring their wealth into the kingdom work.

There are too many young preachers today, young women and men, who refuse to work on wealth building. That is how we were deceived when we first started. We were told we do not need to build wealth because Jesus is coming tomorrow. However, I am here to tell you He is not coming tomorrow.

See, that is the problem. The problem is we have been taught we do not need to work on building wealth because we are kingdom people! In order to maintain the people that are going to be brought from the other side you have to build wealth. However, you also have to go over there and get the wealth by strategy.

Issachar calls the people to the mountain. That is what happens here. He is a strong person but when he gets peace he can become lazy. He looks at all of his abundance and says, "Ah, I am at peace, what do I need? I do not have need. I am satisfied. There is joy here. It is pleasant. Let's just enjoy ourselves and have heavenly frolickings. Let's go dancing on the mountains of heaven and not do any business here on earth."

Young people have to understand this. Wealth building

is going to be important for the next move of God. Issachar called the people to the mountain. However, he also called them to make sacrifices and to do some trading up in the mountain, in the spirit and not below. He called them to trade at a different and higher level.

TIMES SEASONS AND TRADING

There is something else about Issachar. The Bible says he knew the times and knew what Israel must do. Issachar is a spirit of discerning the times.

We need to study how markets move. We need to study how economies move so that we can begin to invest as a people, as the body of

> **"** There are seasons when time dilates. When time dilates, it is for the birthing of something new. **"**

Christ, in order to produce the wealth that does the work of the kingdom. In this heaven, it is all about building the throne, building weaponry and pathways of traveling back, in and out. It is about allowing the flow and releasing people who have the gifting from the world of darkness to come into this kingdom world, bringing their gift with them. It is about releasing the captured wealth back and then trading at a higher level in terms of the mountain. Not trading based on your emotion.

I am going to show you an example of what I'm talking about in terms of when you deal with the principles of trading. Why do you think God asked Abraham to go sacrifice his son, Isaac? It is a good Sunday school lesson. Do you know what it means to take your own son? It means you have to release your emotion from your son because he is your greatest attachment. You cannot sacrifice your son without thinking. To trade at a higher level means to trade without emotional attachment. "They shall call the people unto the mountain... to make sacrifices." Kings always make greater sacrifice than the people they rule. If you wonder why kings are always doing better it is because they trade at a higher level.

> " When the Father decides to release His new works on the earth, He doesn't give it to Christians. He gives it into the atmosphere. "

If you always trade with an emotional attachment it brings your trading down to the level of Reuben and your first level issues. It is not easy. Nobody said it was easy. If it was easy, everybody would be doing it. First, you have to understand that, as a king, you are being called to the mountain.

Your mountain is a mountain where you make sacrifices and trade. Issachar is going to make sure you understand the times. It's not just the sacrifice, it is not just the trading but it's the timing of the trading. Do you know how hard it is to be a thinker and to trade at the right time? Do you know how hard it is to be an emotional person and to trade at the right time? Both thinking and emotion can become your hindrance in the area of trading. That is why you move to the next level of thinking, which transfers you to the next place you are desiring.

A KING MUST KNOW THE TIMES

Dealing with Issachar is the principle of the mastering of time. A king must master time. How do you master time? Right now, you are only in the middle. You have not got though the full 12 Lower Dimensions. You have not even achieved half of the day. You're just one quarter of a full day. Remember, the 24 hours is a manifestation of heaven. The 24 hours of the day is God giving you a symbol of heaven, of the basic heaven (The Lower 12 Dimensions and The Upper 12 Dimension) that man is supposed to experience while on earth and which allows him to experience the wider dimensions. It is your basic experience. It is the basic key to moving in dimensions.

Issachar teaches you how to master time. The Bible says, "They shall call the people unto the mountain; there they shall offer sacrifices of righteousness" (Deut 33:19). Take that verse and then add it to Abraham, who tried offering Isaac on the mountain. Why on the mountain? The mountain always represents the higher places, the upper heaven. The mountain signifies other dimensions. I heard people say it represents authority, and that is true. However, the first thing a mountain represents is a high place. It is the higher place, which represents the "Upper 12 Dimension". So how do you get into the upper heavenly realm?

You have to understand the timing of doing activity because everything is not done simultaneously at every time on earth. Remember, we are dealing with the earthly. The lower level heavens which are controlled, are time-oriented. They are time-oriented because they deal with you going through your personal life cycles and dealing with things inside of you. You have limited time to 'do'. Therefore, when you get to Issachar and to kingship, you must understand how time functions and be able to do things in their right time and in their right place. This area is the area of wealth creating. I cannot over-emphasize this.

Creating wealth is based on understanding times and seasons. The principle of wealth in the lower heaven (Lower 12 Dimension) fluctuates with the movement of time. That is why the economic cycles go up, go down, go up, go down. If you do not have the capacity of the discernment of time you will always struggle. This is why Issachar is placed with Judah. This is why there are three dimensions joined together. It is because this is where you begin to operate in kingship.

You are not a king simply because you see a throne. You are a king because you have the insight and the capacity to draw wealth, know when wealth is rising and to know how to attract it to yourself when it is the right time.

The Issachar dimension is this place. This is Ecclesiastes chapter 3. The whole chapter of Ecclesiastes tells us that to everything there is a time and there is a season. To everything! Not to some things. Everything that is written in this Scripture is an illustration, an example. But it is not the complete list. It's not an exhaustive list of things that have times and seasons. Money has times and seasons. That is why Scripture says money takes wings and flies (Prov 23:5).

You need to understand these things. It is a problem if you do not understand how to function in the natural or how the natural works. The natural you're dealing with is time constrained. Eternity is not. So at a very specific moment, based on where you are, there is a gate that opens into eternity. We are going to deal with that later but here you get an understanding from God how to function. God gives you the capacity to read the times.

This is what Daniel, Shadrach, Meshach, and Abednego had. They had the capacity to know the times. The Bible says, "The sons of Issachar understood the times" (1 Chronicles 12:32). There are two different words for time in Hebrew. The word that matters is that word 'Aleph Tau', which is "at." This indicates the circle of eternity that allows time to be opened up enough for those who have eyes to see to get what is available.

TIME DILATIONS AND NEW WORKS

There are seasons when time dilates. When time dilates, it is for the birthing of something new. The problem is, people who call themselves spirit-filled believers don't have a clue about times and seasons because they're so busy talking about their spirituality. Nobody among them is actually creating something new. When was the last time you met a born-again believer who invented something new, apart from just talking about going to heaven, having experiences in heaven, and telling you what they understand about God.

There are specific seasons when there are time dilations. Sometimes when the time dilates, some people get caught up in the time dilation and have experiences and receive things that are coming into the natural dimension from the supernatural, from the eternal dimension. This is because they just happen to be in the right place at the right time, or they just happen to be thinking the right thought. However, if you train yourself, you can actually know when these things are coming and prepare yourself to receive and to attract them to yourself.

When the Father decides to release His new works on the earth, He doesn't give it to Christians. He gives it into the atmosphere. Christians are always thinking it is given to them. If it was being given to Christians, the person who invented the iPhone would have been a Christian. At a time when Steve Jobs and Bill Gates were doing their computer work, there was an opening in the heavenly realm for the whole world. The funny thing is, very few Christians and people who love God ever get involved.

Do you even realize that all this talking about your spirituality is a hindrance to your capacity to receive from heaven? We teach 'this', teach 'that' and nobody seems to be getting it. We have Christian scientists who, instead of creating something new, are busy trying to convince the world that the earth was created in seven literal days.

What does that have to do with anything? Is it going to feed the hungry? Is it going to remove world hunger? Is it going to stop sickle cell anemia? We are kings and queens in the kingdom. We are kings for God's sake. We are priests. However, we have not tapped into the Issachar dimension.

We do not know how time works because we do not study nature. We do not even study the stars. Some people say, "Oh no, that is demonic." However, God did not make the stars in the sky to oppress us. They are not conspiring against us.

Keep in mind that this is a heavenly dimension where most believers get caught up in their own hubris. It's a dimension of rest and the dimension of self-satisfaction. This is a dimension of spiritual lullaby. You know that is what the father said about Issachar. He said Issachar is a strong donkey who was lying down between two burdens. That is right. He saw that rest was good and he lay down, put his shoulder to the burden and became a slave.

Do you know what this means? You become addicted to your experience of heaven without production - like taking hashish / marijuana. It is just that this hashish is 'experiencing God' because you are not producing anything. You're just sitting around and singing a Christian version of "Puff the magic dragon, lived by the sea..."

When it says Issachar is a stubborn donkey - opinionated,

self-aggrandizing, self-affirming, without anything to prove or offer - we must be careful. Sometimes, what we think is knowledge of God can really make us so drunk with ourselves, with our personal experience, that we actually think we know God, when all we know is ourselves.

FRUIT IS CONCRETE!

Let's try this again. "Ye shall know them by their fruits" (Matt 7:16). Can I mess up your theology just a little bit?

Most of you think that "by their fruits you shall know them" means that I did not commit fornication today - therefore I am a good person. I did not lie today. I did not covet something big today. So you count everything you did not do. Then you think "I've got fruit!" However, do you realize what happens with the fruit God is talking about?

God's fruit is the creation of the earth and the universe. A fruit is a concrete creation of something new. The possibility and potential for transforming the future - genetically, intrinsically, whatever. So what have we produced? It's amazing how much Christians sit around arguing about who's right and who's wrong. It's all about doctrine. It's not about producing anything. Why are Pentecostals screaming and shouting about whether Holy Spirit is a male or a female or whether Holy Spirit speaks in French or English etc.?

The Mormons are busy building and creating new things, buying up hotel chains, building things. You stay in their hotel every day when you travel while you're busy arguing about

> **"** It is because it is a way of creating a capacity to align with what is coming and being transferred to the earth. **"**

who's right theologically. Your theology is not directing you to where you're supposed to go in order to produce the things you're supposed to produce. So once you argue your theology right, you go back to sleep. We argue ourselves to weariness and then we go back to sleep. We do not produce.

I know I am being quite strong here but there is a creative shining forth coming from God in the next season. That is going to change things. In fact, it is beginning already. However, I am afraid that many are going to be left outside of it. Very few of us will enter because we are so busy doing so much other activity. We can't discern the time.

Do you know why God gave Israel the command to sacrifice during the New Moon and to sacrifice specifically when the star systems were in particular constellations? It is because it is a way of creating a capacity to align with what is coming and being transferred to the earth.

Do you know why early Christians spent early morning in prayer? Most Christians today do not even pray in the morning. They don't even know the hour to pray. That is how the early Christians could change all of the Roman Empire. They took hold of the hours of transition. That is how Korean Christians changed Korea. That is how Nigerian Christians are changing Nigeria. That's how the early European Christians changed Europe. Remember, China was a thousand years ahead of Europe before Europe received Christianity.

Some people would like us to believe that it was Paganism that changed Europe. It was Christianity. They figured out how to control the hours, how to align the hours, how to discern the hours and to know when creative things were coming. People locked themselves up just to receive.

The Bible says the sons of Issachar *knew* what Israel should do. Do you know that David discovered the power of the sons of Issachar and actually put 22,000 of them together? David had over 24 inventions. All he did was sit around and figure out what time it was. Solomon had over 24 businesses. Read it. It is right in the Scriptures. They were not mom and pop operations. They were multi-national companies where things were transported from one nation to another nation that was on the other side of the sea. By the way, that is why Solomon got into so much trouble. His whole thing was to figure out the times, to figure out ways to trade, to figure out the right time to trade, and to figure out how to do things and he turned to Foreign God's to do this.

The Hindus know about this. That is why everywhere they go, they prosper almost more than Christians do. However, it is not for lack of Biblical insight. It is not for lack of God not telling us. It is not for lack of us not having the principles. It's because we are too lazy to think about these things. We want to talk about spiritual matters. "I see fire." Good for you. So? "I see wind blowing." Good for you. So? "Feathers are falling!" So?

Do you realize when feathers fall out of an animal, the feathers are dead? Is that what you want? What does it mean for you to have dead feathers fall from an animal? What does it have to do with anything? Gold dust is not gold. (I think I just lost all my speaking invitations right now - but it is not gold).

Now you talk to me about somebody like my friend in Nigeria, a Muslim who became a Christian. God told him to go to a certain place and buy the land. He bought the land and there's gold. Now he's building the first 10-story prayer tower - the tallest in the world - right in the center of where Christians are getting killed. Now if you tell me about somebody like that, then I will listen to you. This is what I mean by fruit must be concrete.

Why is it that Christians are descending in their wealth scale while Muslims are rising, Hindus are rising and Buddhists are rising? It is because Christians don't take the time to study the times. They are busy waiting for Jesus to come. Every time you turn around you hear, "He's coming soon! He is coming soon! No, no, no, it's not today; it's tomorrow!"

We are on the verge of a great transformation in the globe, in the universe. We are also on the verge of great business ideas being birthed. However, I am scared for people who call themselves Christians, including the nominal Christians. Even the nominal Christians who should know better are also participating in what the 'super-spiritual' Christians are doing. It is a sickness in the Body of Christ. We're busy trying to corrupt each other in things that are irrelevant.

The Issachar Dimension is the capacity to understand time and to access eternity in order to use the time dilation for manifestation in the natural. Nothing comes to this place without a human being. Therefore, you must prepare yourself to receive. If you are still operating in anger, in your lust for recognition or in your self-definition based on identity and association, then you really cannot see when dilation happens.

THE HEAVENS ARE REVEALED ALL AROUND US

When you overcome those issues of the first triad, the first thing God shows you is royalty, your kingship, your rising into Judah. Then He shows you Zebulun. Then He shows you and teaches you how to be Issachar. God brings people around you and takes you to a heavenly realm where you begin to see how time and eternity interact with one another. Time and eternity interact based on the days. They interact based on the hours. They interact based on the weekdays. They interact based on the 28 days of the moon. They interact based on the cycle of life. They interact based on the movement of the sun, on the rotation of the earth and its different positions.

It sounds simple. However, the ancestors of humanity are trying to communicate to you what is already in Scripture. It is everywhere you turn - the symbols of architecture, the symbols of the church are speaking to you. You cannot walk into a traditional church building and not know what the church represents. They built the churches with a strategic purpose.

The greatest thing you can do for yourself is to be observant. Be awake. Be alert. There are so many signs around you that can actually awaken you, keep you awake and make you understand the things that God is doing.

There is a stained glass window in my church building. It is divided into 4 segments - the first world, the second world, the third world, and the fourth world. If you look at the stained glass window, in every fourth segment there are 3 divisions. So there are actually 12. This stained glass window is actually the Tree of Life. People are always communicating these things but we can be so caught up in our own so-called spirituality that we are not listening. Nobody is hiding anything from you. It is just that you're not awake.

I'll explain now what times and seasons are. In Greek mythology there is a god that is an important metaphor for what we are talking about - Kronos, the god of time. Kronos was also the prison keeper of every other god that made a mistake. He caught them and put them in prison in a manner that they could not break out of. Therefore, Kronos is a prison house.

Time is a prison house. There is a constant movement to keep you from getting out of that prison house. That's the basic reason for the shifting of the hours. So you think time is running away from you. You are never able to break out. However, when you get to know the Lord Jesus Christ, you get to know God, and you get to understand who you are.

The sons of Issachar are coming. When people heard my teaching about Issachar years ago it wasn't fully comprehended. "Oh the sons of Issachar, discerning the times." I was just laughing. It is one thing to talk about truth. It is another thing to actually know what is happening. When you become an Issachar - when you understand the sons of Issachar - you understand the times and begin creating new things.

The sons of Issachar are people who understand how to open the prison doors and how to keep the dilation of time open enough so that the things that are being revealed can be seen and be caused to manifest. There is always, in life, the invasion of eternity into time. When the Bible talks about Jesus Christ, it says, "in the fullness of time." It uses that phrase several times. It refers to the alignment of time.

There were about 12 kings from the East who came to greet the birth of the Messiah. They were from Ethiopia, because the Ethiopians have a story about this and because the word "kadem" which is translated 'East', can also mean 'an ancient place'. These kings that were coming were studying the stars to look for the alignment because there was an alignment that allows eternity to invade time in a particular way. These guys were watching and they knew that the alignment had happened. The Scripture says they followed the star. Do you think this is one single star that they are following? That is not what it is. They followed a constellation. The miracle of the movement of the Magi was that the constellation disappeared when they arrived at Herod's place and could not be seen, but it was still up there in the sky.

So how do you do this? How do you access time? First, you need to understand the end of that chapter in Ecclesiastes. "He has put eternity into man's heart." (Eccl 3:11 NAS) It is not out there. It is in here, in your heart. You are starting in the wrong place when you start outside. "He has made everything beautiful in its time." He has made it in such a way that nobody can understand the beginning and the end of His work. Ah! He has placed eternity in our hearts.

> **"** It is so that your DNA can be transformed and you can deal with all that damage. Once you begin to navigate this, God might make you jump from one triad to another. What He wants to do is to have you be tested in the flames of the Seven Spirits of God and come back. **"**

The reason I'm teaching you about heaven is to help you understand the heaven that is in your heart. If you don't understand the heaven in your heart, all that things you're trying to look for out there is a waste of your time. Eternity is not out there. It is hidden in you. That is what Jesus meant when He said the kingdom is in your heart? Which kingdom? It is not the Kingdom of heaven, it is the Kingdom of God. This is why I keep talking about the coming shift in power. It is coming from God.

The Kingdom of God is in every human being. What is not in every human being's heart is heaven. The Kingdom of God allows you to have access to the Kingdom of heaven if you will accept the connection between the two. The Kingdom of heaven belongs to Christ.

To understand the relationship between the Kingdom of God and the Kingdom of heaven is to understand how to align things. The Lower 12 Dimension of the sons of Jacob are the Kingdom of God. It is a heaven but it is God's terrain because it belongs to Israel. It is the Father's terrain. It belongs to the human body and deals with the human body. Until you deal with the human body in the Israel paradigm, you really cannot truly experience the Upper 12 Dimension and above - the Kingdom of heaven and above.

Remember, when you are born again you're engrafted to the tree called Israel. There is a reason you are engrafted. It is so that your DNA can be transformed and you can deal with all that damage. Once you begin to navigate this, God might make you jump from one triad to another. What He wants to do is to have you be tested in the flames of the Seven Spirits of God and come back.

NAVIGATING THE SECOND TRIAD

Let's first deal with Zebulun and Issachar. How is Zebulun parallel to Issachar? Issachar is a carrier of burdens. Remember that Judah, Issachar and Zebulun function in the dimension of the kings. Zebulun is the one who dips his feet in oil, who is the wayfaring person that goes from seashore to seashore. Zebulun is the wayfaring guy that travels in ships, but he's also the one who dips his feet in oil. He's the one who produces wealth and who lives in a place of wealth.

Issachar is a diviner that sees. He is able to discern the times. Why is he paired with Zebulun? Because if you are a sea-faring person, you need to understand times and seasons. It says that Issachar knows what Israel should do. Do you understand that a king and a merchant need to understand the times.

Let's talk about economic issues. Companies and CEOs who do not understand the season go bankrupt. Merchants must understand the times. This is why these guys are involved with psychics, tarot cards, and similar activities - to find out what the season is. That's why kings call astrologers and magicians to discern what the time is. It's all about making profit and having the wealth to do what they need to do, and going to war.

Zebulun is dipped in oil. He's a merchant and an adventurer. He must go, even when it's not warfare. He is moved to go everywhere. He can become a vagabond. So he needs Issachar to restrain him. If you go into the city, you will have a problem. And Issachar himself is also one who creates wealth by not moving.

They both have that wealth issues but Issachar is the tribe that didn't have to really labor. They just threw their seed into the field and, because the field was so fertile, they didn't have to really work like everybody else. They knew the times and they threw their seed into the ground. They produced the greatest harvest because they knew the times. Because they knew how to discern the times, they would help Zebulun in his adventure as a merchant.

Now let's talk about these parallels. Your strength is your weakness. Sometimes your weakness, when harnessed, is your greatest strength. The problem is you want to focus on your strength because you're comfortable with it, so your weakness gets hampered. Your weakness is not really what you think it is. It's not opposite from your strength. If you harness your weakness and look at it in the face and keep facing it until you develop it, it will actually make you stronger. Why does God say, "my strength is made perfect in weakness (2 Cor 12:9)?"

You have been taught to fear your weakness. The truth is, you work on your weakness, you face it, you develop it, and you make sure that you're able to deal with it - until it becomes your strength. When your weakness becomes your strength, you'll put your whole intention into it. Therefore, it is something you intentionally develop. Your strength is something you don't intentionally develop. It's something that is part of your reaction to reality. You rejoice in it, thinking it's something great, but you didn't develop it. It's just a reaction.

People always ask me, "How are you such a great speaker?"

When I was starting out, I was so scared of talking. I always thought I would be wrong about something. But I kept practicing. Even after 25 years of ministry, every time I would get in front of people, I'd go to the bathroom first and throw up. That which you develop intentionally is more powerful than that which you have been given.

I'm not talking about grace now. The strengths that you have make you comfortable and this is what's wrong with many Christians. They are comfortable with their strength and never try to transmute their weakness into strength.

As they are in your life, so they are in the universe. The uninhabitable universe is paralleled by those that are in the inhabitable, but they communicate with one another. The sun is parallel to the moon and they need one another. They can mutually destroy each other, but they also need one another. The man needs the woman, but when their desire to become opposite is strong they can mutually destroy each other, or they can come together and work and produce something. They're not as far apart as they think they are.

GLOSSARY OF TERMS

The following is a list of terms used in the book that some readers may not be familiar with.

The Binary Principle is a law of creation based on the numerical value of 10. The Binary Principle shows that the expansive and contractive nature of creation propagates itself in an organized pattern through the values of Zero and One.

The System of Cain is based on the Reptilian Agenda, often referenced to as the 'fallen ones'. It does not directly relate to one particular species but rather represents covenantal systems whom stand against God.

Monster DNA and DNA Dark Spots may be further defined by some, however in this context they may be understood as behavioral and spiritual biases based on genetic inheritance.

The Ecology of the Nested Heavens illustrates the series of connected layers of Heaven. As a multidimensional reality, Heaven is not just one place; it exists as heavens upon heavens upon heavens.

Engaging the Four Faces An example exercise may be using the Name of God "Yod Hey Vav Hey" in chanting to rotationally engage the four faces of the Lion, Ox, Eagle and Man.

The Judgment Room of God, different from the Court room of God, is open only seldom times in creation. This is a place where God releases his judgments, which are not easily reversed. One should not desire for God to sit on his Throne of Judgment, but rather for his Throne of Mercy.

Kabbalah is a traditional Jewish spirituality given through spiritual apprenticeship.

THE DIFFERENT TRIBE ORDERS THROUGH SCRIPTURE

GENESIS 49	NUMBERS 2	REVELATION 7
REUBEN	JUDAH	JUDAH
SIMEON	ISSACHAR	REUBEN
LEVI	ZEBULUN	GAD
JUDAH	REUBEN	ASHER
ZEBULUN	SIMEON	NAPHTALI
ISSACHAR	GAD	MANASSEH
DAN	EPHRAIM	SIMEON
GAD	MANASSEH	LEVI
ASHER	BENJAMIN	ISSACHAR
NAPHTALI	DAN	ZEBULUN
JOSEPH	ASHER	JOSEPH
BENJAMIN	NAPHTALI	BENJAMIN

The order and names of the tribes differ throughout the Scriptures, and thus also in our diagrams. Above is a comparison of the 3 major lists we use in this book.

Genesis 49 is Jacob blessing his sons, and thus their tribes, in birth order. There are 12, and one unnumbered, Dinah. Dinah is the 13th, the Messianic Principle.

In Numbers, over 400 hundred years later, Levi has become the priest and is not counted among the tribes (Num 1: 47-49). Levi becomes the 13th, the Messianic Principle. The tribe of Joseph has been split up between his two sons Ephraim and Manasseh, maintaining the 12 tribes. This was made legal when Jacob owned them as his own sons. "And now thy two sons, Ephraim and Manasseh, which were born unto thee in the land of Egypt before I came unto thee into Egypt, are mine; as Reuben and Simeon, they shall be mine." (Gen 48:5)

In Revelation 7, written about 1300 years after Numbers, we see Levi has been restored to the tribe list. Levi has fulfilled his role as a prophetic metaphor as the Messiah has come and the Levitical priesthood completed. Two tribes are now missing that have been present in the previous lists - Dan and Ephraim. They have both been removed because of their trading and can now only be brought back in by the door of Christ, like a gentile.

Ephraim: "Ephraim is joined to idols: let him alone". (Hosea 4:17)

Dan: "The sons of Dan set up for themselves the graven image; and Jonathan, the son of Gershom, the son of Manasseh, he and his sons were priests to the tribe of the Danites until the day of the captivity of the land." (Judges 18:30 NAS)

"So the king consulted, and made two golden calves, and he said to them, "It is too much for you to go up to Jerusalem; behold your gods, O Israel, that brought you up from the land of Egypt." He set one in Bethel, and the other he put in Dan. Now this thing became a sin, for the people went *to worship* before the one as far as Dan." (1 Kings 12:28-30 NAS)

Note, the "king" mentioned here is Jeroboam, of the tribe of Ephraim!

ABOUT THE AUTHOR

AACTEV8 International was founded by Adonijah Ogbonnaya (ATC, BA, MA Theol, MA, PhD Theol, PhD Bus. Publishing) and Benedicta Ogbonnaya as a Church Planting and Christian Education Service located in Venice, California. After twenty-five years in ministry, the Lord called Dr. Ogbonnaya in 2001 to expand his Ministry to allow full participation in the Fivefold Ministry by the total body of Christ. In 2003, Dr. Ogbonnaya moved into Apostolic Ministry by opening congregations and ministerial centers and holding meetings around the globe. Dr. Ogbonnaya is the founder and CEO of AACTEV8 International and is recognized as one of the foremost revelational Biblical teachers of our time. He has impacted the lives of hundreds of thousands of people nationally and internationally. AACTEV8's founder has published books and multi-media collections that have transformed many around the world.

HASHAMAYIM 1B AND 2

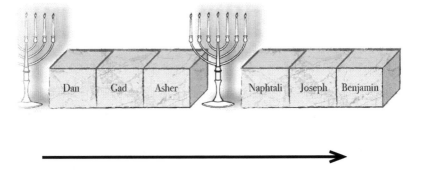

HaShamayim 1B will continue the revelation of the structures of the heavens, especially the 3rd and 4th triads of the Lower '12' Dimension.

HaShamayim 2 will go deeper into the protocols for navigating and accessing the heavenly dimensions and the powers and possibilities embedded within them.

Seraph Creative

Heaven's Heart for Earth

Seraph Creative is a collective of artists, writers, theologians & illustrators who desire to see the body of Christ grow into full maturity, walking in their inheritance as Sons Of God on the Earth.

Sign up to our newsletter to know about the release of the next book in the series, as well as other exciting releases.

Visit our website :
www.seraphcreative.org

21330853R00165

Printed in Great Britain
by Amazon